CO-AYF-473

The Schoolyard Game

The Schoolyard Game

An Anthology of Basketball Writings

Edited by Dick Wimmer

Macmillan Publishing Company
New York
Maxwell Macmillan Canada
Toronto
Maxwell Macmillan International
New York *Oxford* *Singapore* *Sydney*

3 1172 03265 7694

Copyright © 1993 by Dick Wimmer

All rights reserved. No part of this book may be reproduced or transmitted in any form or by any means, electronic or mechanical, including photocopying, recording, or by any information storage and retrieval system, without permission in writing from the Publisher.

Macmillan Publishing Company
866 Third Avenue
New York, NY 10022

Maxwell Macmillan Canada, Inc.
1200 Eglinton Avenue East, Suite 200
Don Mills, Ontario M3C 3N1

Macmillan Publishing Company is part of the Maxwell Communication Group of Companies.

Library of Congress Cataloging-in-Publication Data

The Schoolyard game : an anthology of basketball writings/
edited by Dick Wimmer.
p. cm.
ISBN 0-02-630162-8
1. Basketball stories. 2. American fiction. 3. Basketball.
I. Wimmer, Dick.
PS648.B39S35 1993 92-33762
810.8'0355—dc20

Reprint permissions will be found on pages 203–205.

Macmillan books are available at special discounts for bulk purchases for sales promotions, premiums, fund-raising, or educational use. For details, contact:

Special Sales Director
Macmillan Publishing Company
866 Third Avenue
New York, NY 10022

10 9 8 7 6 5 4 3 2 1

Printed in the United States of America

LIT.
810.8
S372

For my grandmother,

who couldn't dribble

493

Contents

CONTENTS

CONTENTS

Acknowledgments

I'd like the thank my editor, Rick Wolff, and his assistant, Rob McMahon, for all their unflagging support and encouragement; my longtime buddy, Hal Richman; my sons; and dear, sweet Tory.

Introduction

Listen now to the sounds of the court on hardwood, blacktop, or concrete: the sneakers' squeal and squeak, ball's rubber thump and rhythmic patter—how many hours shooting alone on my sloping drive with the play-by-play whirling joyously inside my head, straining hard to be fair, yet have my heroes win—and later on as a teenager, entering fabled arenas blazing with light as all those images sprang into life: Cousy or Davies, Oscar or Wilt, or—Pistol Pete racing full speed up the glistening floor with his floppy hair and sloppy socks to stop time in mid-dribble by flipping the ball before him with his right hand, as though to pass left, then slapping it blindly with his left hand to his cutting teammate on the right; or like a thoroughbred bursting out of the starting gate with gusto, Magic on the front end of a fast-break, Scott and Worthy filling the lanes, and, as he nears the basket, freezing the defenders—who assume he'll take it to the hoop himself—but suddenly delighting us all into astonished grins with the totally unexpected fake and over-the-shoulder no-look pass to Cooper (where'd he come from?) for the Monster Jam; or the long and breathless pause (though shorter than a home run or football bomb) as Larry Bird, finally weaving free on the parquet floor, softly launches a high-arching, game-deciding three-pointer with a feathery flick of his wrist—that descends in a slow-motion straight line and tickles the twine, nothing but net, as it swishes cleanly through.

Shimmering images too of soaring glides above the rim, a balletic grace in sharp and sweaty contrast with the bruising and cursing collisions under the basket. From makeshift courts before the garage, pickup games at the Y, high school, college, to the NBA, we've all heard the poets of play-by-play, from Marty Glickman's "Boryla bombs," Chick Hearn's "No harm, no foul," Marv Albert's "Frazier with the spin move down the lane—*Yes!*" to even Dick Vitale's hysterical *"Take a T.O., baby, take a T.O.!"* These are the sounds that shaped our images.

But there were writers besides, from Updike to Conroy, Halberstam to McPhee, turning out brilliant basketball prose. So listen now with your eyes and mind as you sift through and savor the richest collection that I could find.

The Schoolyard Game

John Edgar Wideman

From "Michael Jordan Leaps the Great Divide"

When it's played the way it's spozed to be played, basketball happens in the air, the pure air; flying, floating, elevated above the floor, levitating the way oppressed peoples of this earth imagine themselves in their dreams, as I do in my lifelong fantasies of escape and power, finally, at last, once and for all, free. For glimpses of this ideal future game we should thank, among others, Elgin Baylor, Connie Hawkins, David Thompson, Helicopter Knowings, and of course, Julius Erving, Dr. J. Some venerate Larry Bird for reminding us how close a man can come to a perfect gravity-free game and still keep his head, his feet firmly planted on terra firma. Or love Magic Johnson for confounding boundaries, conjuring new space, passing lanes, fast-break and break-down lanes neither above the court nor exactly on it, but somehow whittling and expanding simultaneously the territory in which the game is enacted. But really, as we envision soaring and swooping, extending, refining the combat zone of basketball into a fourth, outer, other dimension, the dreamy ozone of flight without wings, of going up and not coming down till we're good and ready, then it's Michael Jordan we must recognize as the truest prophet of what might be possible.

John Updike

From Rabbit, Run

Boys are playing basketball around a telephone pole with a backboard bolted to it. Legs, shouts. The scrape and snap of Keds on loose alley pebbles seems to catapult their voices high into the moist March air blue above the wires. Rabbit Angstrom, coming up the alley in a business suit, stops and watches, though he's twenty-six and six three. So tall, he seems an unlikely rabbit, but the breadth of white face, the pallor of his blue irises, and a nervous flutter under his brief nose as he stabs a cigarette into his mouth partially explain the nickname, which was given to him when he too was a boy. He stands there thinking. The kids keep coming, they keep crowding you up.

His standing there makes the real boys feel strange. Eyeballs slide. They're doing this for themselves, not as a show for some adult walking around town in a double-breasted cocoa suit. It seems funny to them, an adult walking up the alley at all. Where's his car? The cigarette makes it more sinister still. Is this one of those going to offer them cigarettes or money to go out in back of the ice plant with him? They've heard of such things but are not too frightened; there are six of them and one of him.

The ball, rocketing off the crotch of the rim, leaps over the heads of the six and lands at the feet of the one. He catches it on the short bounce with a quickness that startles them. As they stare hushed he sights squinting through blue clouds of weed smoke, a suddenly dark silhouette like a smokestack against the afternoon spring sky, setting his feet with care, wiggling the ball with nervousness in front of his chest, one widespread white hand on top of the ball and the other underneath, jiggling it patiently to get some adjustment in air itself. The cuticle moons on his fingernails are big. Then the ball seems to ride up the right lapel of his coat and comes off his shoulder as his knees dip down, and it appears the ball will miss because though he shot from an angle the ball is not going toward the backboard. It was not aimed there. It drops into the circle of the rim, whipping the net with a ladylike whisper. "Hey!" he shouts in pride.

"Luck," one of the kids says.

"Skill," he answers, and asks, "Hey. O.K. if I play?"

There is no response, just puzzled silly looks swapped. Rabbit takes off his coat, folds it nicely, and rests it on a clean ashcan lid. Behind him the dungarees begin to scuffle again. He goes into the scrimmaging thick of them for the ball, flips it from two weak grubby-knuckled child's hands, has it in his own. That old stretched-leather feeling makes his whole body go taut, gives his arms wings. It feels like he's reaching down through years to touch this tautness. His arms lift of their own and the rubber ball floats toward the basket from the top of his head. It feels so right he blinks when the ball drops short, and for a second wonders if it went through the hoop without riffling the net. He asks, "Hey whose side am I on?"

In a wordless shuffle two boys are delegated to be his. They stand the other four. Though from the start Rabbit handicaps himself by staying ten feet out from the basket, it is still unfair. Nobody bothers to keep score. The surly silence bothers him. The kids call monosyllables to each other but to him they don't dare a word. As the game goes on he can feel them at his legs, getting hot and mad, trying to trip him, but their tongues are still held. He doesn't want this respect, he wants to tell them there's nothing to getting old, it takes nothing. In ten minutes another boy goes to the other side, so it's just Rabbit Angstrom and one kid standing five. This boy, still midget but already diffident with a kind of rangy ease, is the best of the six; he wears a knitted cap with a green pompom well down over his ears and level with his eyebrows, giving his head a cretinous look. He's a natural. The way he moves sideways without taking any steps, gliding on a blessing: you can tell. The way he waits before he moves. With luck he'll become in time a crack athlete in the high school; Rabbit knows the way. You climb up through the little grades and then get to the top and everybody cheers; with the sweat in your eyebrows you can't see very well and the noise swirls around you and lifts you up, and then you're out, not forgotten at first, just out, and it feels good and cool and free. You're out, and sort of melt, and keep lifting, until you become like to these kids just one more piece of the sky of adults that hangs over them in the town, a piece that for some queer reason has clouded and visited them. They've not forgotten him: worse, they never heard of him. Yet in his time Rabbit was famous through the country; in basketball in his junior year he set a B-league scoring record that in his senior year he broke with a record that was not broken until four years later, that is, four years ago.

He sinks shots one-handed, two-handed, underhanded, flat-footed, and out of the pivot, jump, and set. Flat and soft the ball lifts. That his touch still lives in his hands elates him. He feels liberated from long gloom. But his body is weighty and his breath grows short. It annoys him, that he gets winded. When the five kids not on his side begin to groan and act lazy, and a kid he accidentally knocks down gets up with a blurred face and walks away, Rabbit quits readily. "O.K.," he says. "The old man's going."

To the boy on his side, the pompon, he adds, "So long, ace." He feels grateful to the boy, who continued to watch him with disinterested admiration after the others grew sullen, and who cheered him on with exclamations: "God. Great. Gee."

Rabbit picks up his folded coat and carries it in one hand like a letter as he runs. Up the alley. Past the deserted ice plant with its rotting wooden skids on the fallen loading porch. Ashcans, garage doors, fences of chicken-wire caging crisscrossing stalks of dead flowers. The month is March. Love makes the air light. Things start anew; Rabbit tastes through sour aftersmoke the fresh chance in the air, plucks the pack of cigarettes from his bobbling shirt pocket, and without breaking stride cans it in somebody's open barrel.

Pat Conroy

From The Great Santini

The challenge match was set for five o'clock that afternoon. Ben swept off the cement court that spread from the back porch of the house to the garage. While Bull dressed upstairs, the rest of the family gathered by the side of the court to cheer Ben while he warmed up. Matt fed Ben passes out beyond the foul line, and Ben, dribbling twice, would fake a drive toward the basket, then go up with a quick awkward jump shot that was adequate even though it lacked artistry and the essential purity of flow always found in good jump shooters. Then he began to drive all the way to the basket, dribbling slowly, then exploding toward the basket, changing hands in midair and letting the ball roll off his fingertips and into the basket.

Lillian coached him from a wicker chair by the porch. "You can't listen to him, Ben. Once you listen to him, he has you beaten. Keep your mind on the game. Your game. And don't worry about him. If you start beating him, he'll start to cheat. You just concentrate on your game."

Bull appeared on the back porch wearing a sweat suit with "United States Marine Corps" stenciled on it. Standing on the porch, he raised his clasped hands over his head and pranced like a boxer going into the ring.

"Boo, booo," his wife and children jeered.

"You ready to go one on one, Dad?" Ben called from under the basket.

"With you?" Bull said, skipping lightly down the stairs. "You ain't man enough to go one on one against the Great Santini."

"Let me play too, Dad," Matt pleaded.

"Naw, you get out of here, Matt. Go sit under a toadstool or something," Bull said. Matt ran into the house. Only Mary Anne saw that he was crying and she followed him. Ben threw a pass to his father. Dribbling three times with both his right and left hand, Bull went into a strangely graceful crouch and threw up an arcing two-hand set shot that swished through the net. Bull crowed with delight, a self-indulgent but euphoric eruption that silenced his wife's catcalls for the moment. Looking toward Lillian, he said, "The old boy's still got it, huh, Petunia?"

"That shot went down with the Titanic, Dad," Ben teased.

"It still counts two points, does it not, jocko?" Bull snapped back, shooting another arcing set that hit the back of the rim and bounced back to him without ever touching the court. Mary Anne slipped out of the back door without Matt and sat down again by her mother. Bull shot another time and once more the ball swished through the net.

"What was it like, Dad," Ben said, throwing him the ball, "shooting at a peach basket?"

"You're gonna find out what it was like having a fist stuck up your left nostril if you don't quit your yappin'."

Mary Anne squealed from the sidelines, "You could stick two fists and a leg up Ben's left nostril with that schnozz of his."

"Ha, ha, very funny," Ben sneered at his sister.

"I'm surprised Mommy let her sweet little boy play any nasty sports at all when the Big Dad was overseas," Bull taunted.

"Don't listen to him, Ben. He's starting on you now. Just think about the game," Lillian called out.

"There's a reason I'm going to beat you, Dad."

"Do tell, sportsfans."

"It's because," and here Ben paused, ensuring that everyone was listening, "it's because you're getting fat."

"What'd you say?" Bull had picked the ball up and was holding it in the crook of his left arm.

Lillian doubled up with laughter in the white wicker chair.

"Not real fat. Just kind of chunky. You look kind of slow now, Dad."

"We'll see who's slow. I told you never to mess with greased lightning, son."

"Greased lightning don't weigh no two hundred twenty pounds."

"I could eat you for breakfast, sportsfans."

"You been eating somethin' real big for breakfast, that's for sure."

Bull threw up another set shot. It was good. Then he looked toward Ben with hard eyes. "Your mouth has improved since I left, but you're still a mama's boy. You still haven't developed the killer instinct. I could psych you out even if I was a hundred years old. If I was paralyzed from the neck down I could still beat you in a spitting contest. And there's one thing we both know. I'm a hell of a lot better athlete than you."

That was true, Ben thought. The sons of Bull Meecham lived with the awareness that they would never match the excellence of their father in athletics. In all sports, they lacked his inextinguishable fierceness, his hunger for games. It was not that they were not competitive; they were, compulsively so. It was that this sense of competition was not elevated to a higher level. In Bull Meecham, the will to win transformed all games into a furious art form. The game was a framework in which there was a winner and a loser. Bull Meecham was always the winner. He played cow bingo with the same fervor as he played his last college basketball game at Saint Luke's. He played Old Maid with Karen and Matt with the same competitiveness as when he battled Japanese pilots in the Pacific. The stakes could be higher in some games than others, but Bull played them all to win. Ben had inherited his father's speed afoot, his good eyes, and much of the competitiveness, but he had not received his father's genius for games, the raw nerve ends and synapses that brought a game up from a region of sport into a faith based on excellence, a creed toughened by fire. But on this hot August day in Ravenel, South Carolina, under the blaze of a terrible sun, Ben thought that he had a great equalizer working for him, called youth.

Ben was five feet ten inches tall and weighed 165 pounds; his father was six feet four inches tall and weighed 220 pounds. But Ben had been correct when he observed that

Bull had thickened over the last years. He had become heavy in the thighs, stomach, and buttocks. The fast places had eroded. Rolls of fat encircled him and he wore the sweat suit to keep his new ballast unexposed. He was planning to lose weight anyway. There was nothing Bull Meecham hated worse than a fat Marine.

It took a long time for Bull to warm up and it gave Ben a chance to study his moves. Lillian called from the sidelines for Bull to "quit stalling." But Bull remained unhurried, gliding around the court with the definitive moves of the natural. Though his speed was gone, his quickness was not. His hands were still very fast. He could handle a basketball with remarkable dexterity for one who had abandoned the court so long ago. He was heavy yet he was still a dancer and the easy moves of the old predator came back to him effortlessly as he went from spot to spot testing his eye.

"Let's get the game going," Lillian said, clapping her hands.

But Bull would not be hurried. He was seriously practicing his two-hand set shot. The hands that could make jets perform exotic gymnastics in the sky had a softness of touch and an inborn surety that made him an excellent outside shooter. The pilot with the good eyes for spotting enemy troop movements, for columns of tanks, and for artillery positions could also use those eyes for looking up, and for judging the distance between the basket and his hands, for that silent worship of rims. He shot his two-hand set in a soft, spinning arc that, when true, snapped through the net in a swishing voice that is the purest music of the game. Even when he missed, the spin on the ball made it die on the rim and it would often bounce once or twice between the rim and the backboard before falling in. As Ben fed him passes from under the basket, Bull made eight out of twelve shots, moving in a semicircle outside the scratched-out foul line. Time after time, Bull brought the ball to eye level, almost resting it on his nose. He sighted the rim, bent his knees, and in a rhythm that never changed launched his body, his arms, and the ball upward toward the basket, his fingers spreading out like fans with the two index fingers pointing toward the center of the rim. Like all good shooters, the pattern of Bull's shooting did not deviate; in fact it was unconscious, buried in instinct, and rooted in long hours of boyhood practice. He did the same thing each time the ball left his fingers to hunt the chords. Over and over, monotonous, without change, until finally he said to his son, "Let's play ball."

"You sure you don't want to warm up for a little longer?" Lillian said. "You've only taken about an hour."

"Do any of you creeps realize that this is not exactly a world-important event?" Mary Anne said.

"Uh, oh," Bull answered, "Miss Funeral Shroud has come to spread joy."

"Don't give him a clear shot, Ben," Lillian coached. "Keep him away from the basket and don't let him take his set."

"Someone ought to cheer for Daddy," Karen said.

"You cheer for him," her mother answered.

"Yeah, Karen, give your Big Dad a few cheers. All the raspberries are coming his way."

"You take it out first, Dad," Ben said, bouncing the ball to his father. "Play to ten baskets by one. You have to win by two."

"Two? Why not one? First guy to ten," Bull protested. "Of course, it's not gonna be that close, sportsfans."

"You have to take it behind the foul line after each shot, Dad."

"Don't stand under the basket, jocko. You might get killed by one of my shots crashing through the basket."

"If you get a shot off."

Ben moved in close to guard his father, who began dribbling toward the basket with deliberate caution. He turned his butt toward Ben and backed toward the basket, dribbling first to the right, then to the left. When Ben tried to reach around to swat at the ball, Bull prevented this by holding him off with his free arm. He took Ben almost underneath the basket, then in a quick, fluid move, he pivoted for a hook shot that caromed lightly off the backboard.

"One to goose egg, sportsfans," Bull shouted at his booing family.

Taking the ball behind the foul line, Ben saw that his father was not coming out to play defense on him. He made a move for the basket, went up for a jump shot. His father, off balance, poked him in the stomach as he went up, but the ball went in.

"He's starting to cheat," Lillian cried out.

"One to one," Ben said.

Bull did not even dribble this time. He set himself immediately and before Ben could recover had launched a high two-hander toward the rim that missed. Rebounding the ball quickly, Ben brought it past the foul line, changed the direction of his dribble twice, gave his father a head fake, a stutter step, then drove toward the basket as recklessly as he knew how. To his surprise, he had broken completely free and laid the ball in effortlessly. "Two to one," he called to his father.

The game became rough. Sweat poured down Bull's face

and Ben caught an elbow under the left eye when he tried to block one of Bull's hook shots. Each time Bull received the ball he would take his time, dribbling cautiously, moving backward, taking his smaller son under the basket. Ben, for his part, kept driving past his father, changing speeds, and sweeping past him as Bull lunged heavily after a son who had fooled him, betrayed him with speed.

Ben kept saying to himself, "I'll make him work on defense. I'll get his legs tired trying to stop me. When his legs go, his shooting will go. He's out of shape. If I can't get him tired, I'll get him mad. If I can get him mad, I'll beat him."

The game remained close, both combatants missing shots they should have made and sinking baskets that defied all principles of the game. Finally the score was tied nine to nine, and the family on the sidelines readied themselves for a denouement. Bull had the ball.

Ben pressed in close to him with his left hand waving in front of his father's eyes. He wanted to be sure to prevent the two-handed set. During the game, over and over again, he had proven that Bull was no longer fast enough to drive around him. Bull was breathing as though steam engines were working his lungs, his lips were flecked with dried saliva, and sweat was pouring off his body. He made two half-hearted feints toward the basket, hoping to catch Ben off balance and get an unchallenged set shot. But Ben stayed close to him, his chest almost against his father's belly, their sweat commingling and their breaths crossing like two alien winds.

"Have you ever read *Moby Dick*, Dad?" Ben asked.

"Shit, no," Bull murmured, pivoting around and beginning a low, cautious dribble, inching his way toward the basket with Ben fastened to his rump. "Why do you ask, sportsfans?"

"Because you kind of remind me of that great big, fat, white whale."

"Touché, touché," Lillian screamed.

"This looks like the last shot of the game, jocko."

"If you make it," Ben said, leaning with all his weight against his father's rear, trying to slow the inevitable move toward the basket for the easy hook shot.

"Does a maggot live in dead meat?" Bull said.

"God, Dad is disgusting," said Mary Anne.

"He's just low born," said Lillian. Then she began shouting, "Kill him, Ben. Keep your hands up."

At that moment Bull glanced over at Lillian, irritation spliced on the corners of his mouth. When Ben saw his eye depart from the center of action, he stepped backward, like a caboose uncoupling from another car. In that single instant, Ben was unseen and unfelt by his father. He slapped Bull on the left buttock, then swept low around his father's right side. Feeling Ben's release and the hand hitting his left side, Bull reflexively looked to his left and switched the ball to his right hand. As he did so, he realized his mistake and tried to recover, but by this time Ben had flicked the ball away from him and retrieved it near the porch.

The family of spectators broke into applause when they sensed that Ben had a chance to win the game. At the far edge of cement, almost touching the porch, Ben stood motioning for his father to come out to play defense.

"Whip his fanny, Ben," Matt's voice cried out from behind the screen door in the kitchen.

"It is I, the Great Bentini," Ben mimicked as he began to dribble the ball between his legs trying to shame his father into open court where he knew he could drive around him.

"Let's play ball," Bull rumbled, his face blood red from anger. His eyes had narrowed into starpoints of cold, the killing edge of a personal fury that marked a crossing of the line which Lillian recognized immediately.

"Why don't we just call it a tie, and call both of you winners?" she said.

"I said let's play ball," Bull growled in a lower, more frightening octave.

"Why don't you just come out here and get it, Great Santini?" Ben teased, unaware of the changes that were taking place in his opponent.

"I'd quit now, Ben," Mary Anne advised. "He's getting that same look on his face that he gets when he runs over turtles on trips."

Dribbling slowly, Ben started toward his father, changing hands with each dribble, hoping to catch Bull with his weight shifted in the wrong direction. "Do you know, Dad, that not one of us here has ever beaten you in a single game? Not checkers, not dominoes, not softball, nothing."

"C'mon, mama's boy," Bull whispered. "Bring little mama's boy up to Daddy Bull." Right hand, left hand, right hand, left hand, the ball drummed against the cement as Ben waited for his father to move out against him and Bull held back, fearing the drive to the basket. At the foul line, Ben left his feet for the jump shot, eyed the basket at the top of his leap, let it go softly, the wrist snapping, the fingers pointing at the rim and the ball spinning away from him as Bull lunged forward and drove his shoulder into Ben's stomach, knocking him to the ground. Though he did not see the ball go in, he heard the shouts of his mother and sisters; he saw Matthew leaping up and down on the porch. He felt his father rise off him slowly, coming up beaten by a son for the first time in his life. Screaming with joy, Ben jumped up and was immediately flooded by his family, who hugged, slapped, pummeled, and kissed him.

Lillian and Matt tried to pick Ben up, but he was too heavy and all three of them fell into the grass laughing, forgetting the lone figure of the father standing under the basket, sweating, red-faced, and mute, watching the celebration of his wife and children with the inchoate, resurrected anger of a man who never quit in his life. Mary Anne saw him standing alone and went over to say something comforting.

"You played a good game, Dad," she said.

"Get out of here."

"You didn't lose by much," Mary Anne continued, ignoring the vital signs.

"Get out of here before I start knocking every freckle off your face."

Mary Anne put her hands to her face, removed her glasses, and looked at her father with eyes that were filling with tears. "That was mean, Daddy. You had no call to say that," she said, running toward the front yard.

Then Bull shouted at Ben, "Hey, jocko, you gotta win by two baskets."

The backyard became quiet again. Ben looked at his father and said, "You said by one."

"I changed my mind; let's go," Bull said, picking up the basketball.

"Oh, no, Bull," Lillian said, marching toward her husband. "You're not going to cheat the boy out of his victory."

"Who in the hell asked you anything?" Bull said, glaring at his wife.

"I don't care if anybody asked me or not. He beat you fair and square and I'm not going to let you take that away from him."

"Get over here, mama's boy," Bull said, motioning to Ben, "and let's you and me finish this game."

Ben moved forward until he heard his mother shout at him, "You stay right there, Ben Meecham. Don't you dare move."

"Why don't you go hide under your mother's skirts, mama's boy?" Bull said.

He was gaining control of the situation again and was entering a phase of malevolent calm that Lillian was having difficulty translating.

"Mama, I'm gonna play him," Ben said.

"No you're not," his mother answered harshly, with finality, then speaking to her husband, she said, "He beat you, Big Marine. He beat the Big Marine where everybody could see it, right out in the open, and it was beautiful. It was just beautiful. Big Marine can't take it that his baby boy just beat him to death on the basketball court."

"Get in the house, Lillian, before I kick you into the house."

"Don't threaten me, Big Tough Marine. Does Big Tough Marine have to pick on his family the day his son becomes the better man?"

Bull pushed Lillian toward the house, spinning her away from him, and kicked her in the buttocks with a swift vicious kick.

"Stop that, Dad," Ben shouted. "You stop that."

"Quit kicking Mama," Karen screamed.

He kicked her again. Each kick was directing her toward the stairs. Finally, Lillian started to run for the kitchen. Bull would have kicked her another time but Ben got between him and his mother. The screen door slammed as Lillian disappeared from view. Bull's face was hideously contorted as he stood face to face with Ben, who was trembling involuntarily.

"You sort of like winning, don't you, Dad?" Ben said, trying to sound unconcerned and in control, but fear lay heavy on his voice.

Bull went up to Ben until they were almost nose to nose, as Ben had seen Drill Instructors do to recruits. With his forefinger, he began poking Ben's chin. "You get smart with me, jocko, and I'll kick you upstairs with your mother so you pussies can bawl together. Now guard me. You gotta win by two."

"I'm not gonna guard you, Dad. I won," Ben said, his voice almost breaking. He could feel himself about to cry.

Bull saw it too. "That's it, mama's boy. Start to cry. I want to see you cry," Bull roared, his voice at full volume, a voice of drill fields, a voice to be heard above the thunder of jet engines, a voice to be heard above the din of battle. Bull took the basketball and threw it into Ben's forehead. Ben turned to walk into the house, but Bull followed him, matching his steps and throwing the basketball against his son's head at intervals of three steps. Bull kept chanting, "Cry, cry, cry," each time the ball ricocheted off his son's skull. Through the kitchen Ben marched, through the dining room, never putting his hands behind his head to protect himself, never trying to dodge the ball. Ben just walked and with all his powers of concentration rising to the surface of consciousness, of being alive, and of being son, Ben tried not to cry. That was all he wanted to derive from the experience, the knowledge that he had not cried. He wanted to show his father something of his courage and dignity. All the way up the stairs, the ball was hurled against his head. The hair short and bristly from the morning haircut, the head this moment vulnerable, helpless, and loathed. Ben knew that once he made it to his room the ordeal would end, and he would have the night to consider all the symbols of this long march: the heads of sons, the pride of fathers, victors, losers, the faces of kicked wives, the fear of families, the Saturdays in the reign of Santini—but now, now, through this hallway and up these final stairs, I must not cry, I must not cry. Until he saw his room. Breaking into a run, he felt Bull release him, free him, his head throbbing, dizzy; and the son of the fighter pilot fell onto his bed face downward, afraid that tears would come if he did not stem their flow in the cool whiteness of his pillow. His father stood in the doorway and Ben heard him say so that the whole family could hear, "You're my favorite daughter, Ben. I swear to God you're my sweetest little girl."

Then turning toward the door, blinded by water and light, Ben spit back. "Yeah, Dad, and this little girl just whipped you good."

The door slammed.

Robert Greenfield

From Haymon's Crowd

At the other end of the schoolyard the younger men congregate, the sons and nephews, who have come either to sit and watch or to play and argue about the only game that has any meaning at all for them—basketball. On the stone steps that lead up to a set of double doors that are nearly always locked, the experts recline, a copy of the *Daily News* folded beneath them to sit on, a copy of the *Post* open to the line for the evening's games. The odor of their cheap cigars mixes with the smell of sweat as the game goes on, always the game, on and on, an endless round of half-court, seven-basket, three-man contests.

Reed Kreiger sits by the polished metal banister that divides the steps. Its surface has been worn smooth by the thousands of tiny hands that grasp it on the way in and out of school each day. By all rights, Reed Kreiger should be splayed out on the concrete along the fence where the ballplayers arrogantly sprawl. But he is too thin. Unlike his muscled father, his arms and legs are thin. His ankles too. His thinness embarrasses him. It keeps him from ever wearing shorts to the yard or playing on Saturdays, though he spends hours shooting around by himself when no one else is present.

On a day like this, Reed Kreiger is content just to be where he is, at the very epicenter of the universe, the place where news begins and history is made, the schoolyard. Closing his eyes, he lets the throbbing buzz of the conversation and the warm sun transport him. He has no problems.

When he opens his eyes, Reed Kreiger finds himself staring at the largest white man ever to enter the yard. Stooping so as not to ram his head into the iron bar that forms the top of the side gate is a giant, with large, spatulate hands shoved deep into the pockets of a pair of khaki chino pants that are ripped at the knee and a good four inches too short at the ankle. An expanse of hairy calf flashes from above cheap cotton socks. Arms jut out from his sides at odd angles. His head looks as though it was put on with a pipe wrench.

The look on the giant's face gives him away, completely. Reed Kreiger has seen the look before, in the junior high school cafeteria during lunch hour, where the weak quietly give up their nickels and dimes to avoid being beaten to a pulp by those who earn their weekly allowances by preying on others. The big man is terrified.

From his position along the fence, Liddel Gross casts a cold eye over the newcomer. "No way," he says in a hard, flat voice. "No way he can touch the rim. I got a dollar says he can't."

"Bet," Buttsy Klein says quickly, hungry for some action. Then he catches sight of the giant's feet. "Fuckit," he says disgustedly. "He ain't even wearin' Converse."

Converse, the sneaker of the pros, perpetually marked down and for sale on Kings Highway, are the mark of a true ballplayer. Only *shvartzers* can play without the athletic shoe that bears Chuck Taylor's actual signature on the round white disc that hugs the bulge of the anklebone. *Shvartzers*, it is well known in the schoolyard, can play in anything, open-toed sandals, penny loafers, highly polished black alligator shoes. They are exempt. White men *need* Converse.

"We're on next, right?" Liddel asks, already knowing the answer. "I'm gonna take him on. For a goof.

"Hey!" he shouts in the giant's direction. "You wanna play?"

The big man looks around to see whom Liddel is talking to. He paws at the ground, blinking furiously. "S-sure," he says.

"Great." Liddel beams. "You got it."

Then he turns and squints into the sun, his small ferret face gleaming with delight. "This," he mutters so that only those sitting around him can hear, "is gonna be a *pisser*!"

Hooking his fingers into the repetitive octagons of the wire-mesh fence, Liddel Gross turns and stares out into the street. By the fire hydrant, double-parked, sits a familiar fire-engine red convertible. Behind the wheel is an older man. His face is angular, all bone. What can be seen of his body is equally stark, lean, stripped, and sinewy. All morning he has been driving from schoolyard to schoolyard, looking for a game. His sneakers and basketball are in the trunk. Before he can be bothered to take them out, he must be sure that he will be able to find some true competition, a real run.

Liddel Gross waves a tentative hand in greeting but the older man does not respond. His attention has been captured by the big kid near the steps. A player that size in Brighton that Max Trapp does not know? Impossible.

On the first court, the team that has been winning all afternoon casually vanquishes another opponent. They are three-fifths of the squad that dominates the night center year after year, the blue and white braided laces in their Converse attesting to this fact, each lace threaded so that it begins *atop* the bottom eyelet rather than below. Their woolen sweat socks cost a dollar a pair. They are that perfect shade of Clorox yellow that comes only from repeated washings with strong bleach.

Everything about them is perfect. Despite that, when Liddel Gross leads the giant and Buttsy Klein on court to oppose them, he does so with an arrogance that is unmistakable, as though eighteen thousand fans have jammed Madison Square Garden just to see this happen. Liddel begins guarding Mikey DiAngelo by thrusting an outstretched hand into his stomach, signifying that he is prepared to play Mikey head-to-head all over the court. With somewhat less of a flourish, Buttsy picks up Tommy Falcone, called the Falcon, leaving the big man with no choice but to try to contain Sammy Stein, known to all as Sponge. Sponge always wears as many different colored pairs of sweat socks as he can cram into his size twelve sneakers. He can leap like a black man. In the schoolyard, they like to say that he can take a quarter off the backboard and give you change. It is only an expression. Sammy Stein, called Sponge, never gives anyone anything, much less correct change.

Mikey Dee inbounds to the Falcon, who dribbles to the key, waiting for Sponge to make a move. Playing to the spectators on the steps, Sponge head fakes toward the foul line, then bursts toward the basket like a fullback making for the goal line. The Falcon hits him with a high, spinning pass that Sponge catches on his way up. A soft, creamy look takes possession of his face, a half-mad grin that in future years will come to grace police folders and prison files. Everyone on the steps leans forward, anticipating what will happen next.

Sponge is going to jam, smashing the ball downward from above the rim with so much power and authority that Liddel's team will collapse in awe and shock and slink back to the fence, grateful to have escaped with their lives.

As Sponge begins to rise, the giant rouses himself and tries to get back in the game. From the foul line, he takes one long step and then another, the distance between him and his man disappearing as he stumbles forward, an awkward avalanche looking for a city to engulf. At the very last moment, the giant manages to gain control of himself. He launches his body upward in a little pitty-pat leap that is no match for the graceful elevation Sponge gets when he leaves the ground. Still, it is enough.

Hand and ball come together in midair, one descending with force, the other rising with velocity. The ball vectors crazily against the backboard and caroms straight out into the waiting hands of Liddel Gross, who scoops it up and rams it home for an uncontested layup.

Slapping his palms together in celebration, Liddel bounces up and back on the balls of his feet, shouting, "Atta way, big man. Atta way, *keed*." Quickly, he inbounds to Buttsy, who goes up for a long jumper from the right side. Buttsy follows with another from the opposite corner, falling away. Liddel chips in with a long set shot and quickly they are away, four-nothing, the ball bouncing as though it had eyes and a distinct preference for being handled only by them.

Under the basket, another game is going on. Sponge is working over the big man with all the precision of a woodsman trimming a tree. A shot to the ribs. An elbow to the small of the back. A knee in the thigh. Mikey Dee yells at his teammate to play the game, but Sammy Stein is beyond hearing or caring. No one stuffs Sponge and walks away unscathed to talk about it.

The teams trade baskets. With Liddel's squad needing but one to win, Buttsy runs the Falcon into a pick at the foul line and rolls to the hoop. Sponge is forced to come out and pick him up, leaving the big man free under the basket. Liddel flings him the winning pass, the ball transcribing a series of backward pebbled circles in the sunlight. The big man jumps for it, his body turning awkwardly in midair.

From out of nowhere, Sponge comes flying down the lane. He shoves his shoulder in at a point somewhere below the giant's hip, bridging him so that when the big man falls, he comes down ass backward, his huge body striking the concrete with the hard, percussive *whomp!* of an anti-aircraft shell hitting home.

The big man lies on concrete in a pile of bone, elbows bloodied, chest heaving. A ribbon of spit pearls from one corner of his mouth. The whites of his eyes are very large and wild, like those of some thoroughbred waiting to be destroyed after cracking a forelock in the stretch.

"FOUL!" Liddel screams. *"FUCKIN' FOUL!"*

"Let *him* call it!" the Falcon says automatically.

"Call this, *PRICK!*" Liddel explodes, flinging the ball at

Sponge's head. Sponge ducks and the ball slams into Mikey Dee, knocking him to the ground.

Falcon and Liddel leap on each other with the relish of old and practiced opponents. They roll on the ground, chopping punches to each other's heads. They fart and grunt, their clothes scraping horribly along the concrete. Reed Kreiger watches in fascination, unable to move, as a squadron of older men vaults off the steps around him to pull the two apart. Liddel comes off the ground steaming, blood and snot running from his nose. His T-shirt is torn in three places. A row of fresh tooth marks adorns his neck.

"HE BIT ME!" Liddel howls, fingering his wound, trying to push through the cordon of peacemakers to take yet another shot at the Falcon.

"FUCKIN' . . . *FAGGOT!*" he screams. "If you wanted to gimme a hickey, you shoulda asked."

Falcon balls his fist and takes a threatening step toward Liddel. Then he bursts out laughing. "Fuckin' Liddel," he says, shaking his head in wonder.

"Fuckin' Lid-*dell,*" Mikey Dee echoes. "You crazy, man. You know? C'mon. Play the game."

Liddel pulls away from the circle and goes over to the steps, where the giant has resurrected himself into a half-sitting position. Reed sits just by his shoulder, watching.

"Hey?" Liddel asks. "You okay?"

The giant nods. His drooping head is bent, his eyes half-closed. Like some great sunflower, he is wilting in the warm spring sunshine. He tries to speak but is unable to force the words from his mouth. Grasping the smooth metal banister in his hand, he tries to stand. He sinks back down, gasping for air.

"Our ball," Liddel notes encouragingly. "One to go."

The giant shakes his head. "P-p-pick someone else," he stutters. "I'm through."

In a schoolyard where no one sits down unless he has suffered a compound fracture, with the jagged bone piercing the skin as proof, the big man is tired. Overheated. Suffering from fatigue. He is quitting. An unheard-of violation of the code.

Liddel looks at him for a moment in disbelief. Then he scans the steps for a replacement. For one heart-stopping moment, he considers Reed Kreiger. Then he keeps on looking, finally selecting a more suitable sub. When the game begins again, Buttsy Klein immediately hits a long and anti-climactic jump shot to end it. Liddel's team has won.

"Awright!" Liddel says out loud to himself. "All *fuckin'* right!"

Outside the fence, Max Trapp is already gone, in search of better competition. Three blocks away, the old women give up on the sun, fold their canvas weave beach chairs, and set out for home to begin cooking dinner. *Shabbos* is almost over. The sun disappears behind gray and puffy clouds with the dun color and abrasive consistency of steel wool. It is not yet spring. Not yet. The day grows cold.

Rick Telander

From Heaven Is a Playground

At 9:30 P.M. the park is dark and nearly deserted. Standing by the fence is an old man wearing a green cap, a German who comes to the park frequently to watch the games, carrying a radio from which wafts the classical music of Wagner and Beethoven. He seldom speaks, indeed there is no one for him to talk to. He is always alone, content to watch.

Under the first basket there is a bit of commotion as Cameron, a fifteen-year-old park regular with legs as thick as stove pipes, is being taught the rudiments of stuffing. Eight or nine other youths are all trying to explain their personal techniques for palming the ball, approaching the basket, hooking over the rim, returning to the pavement.

Cameron listens to each intently, nodding his head as the points become clear. When the last man is finished Cameron backs up, wipes his hands, and runs at the basket.

At 5′8″ he is an exceptional leaper, but on his first attempt the ball slams into the back of the rim and bounces ten feet in the air. Cameron remains above, hanging on the rim.

Lloyd Hill, who has been walking down the sidewalk, steps through the hole in the fence onto the dark court. He looks up at the body dangling above. "Get off there, boy," he orders. Cameron drops.

Lloyd points back to the free-throw circle. "Now try the dunk again."

Being the master leaper and stuffer of Foster Park, Lloyd's word is a solemn and valuable thing. Cameron backs up and snorts like a bull before charging down the lane. Though he seems to rise beyond all normal boundaries for a man his size, Cameron's second attempt is a repeat of the first, with him again hanging like wash on the rim.

"Don't be scared," says Lloyd. "Man, that first time you gots to overcome. The dunk is something, specially for a little man." He pats Cameron paternally on the head.

"Now I know you is kinda scared of falling over ass-backwards and smacking your head on the floor. But it ain't gonna happen if you just let the ball go once it's over the hole. See, you doing the two-handed power stuff, which is cool because you kinda squatty and all, and so you make the run a little different than if you was hook-dunking or behind-the-head-dunking."

Lloyd simulates a takeoff without leaving the ground. The other players begin dunking the ball to show how it's done, and soon they form two lines as in pregame drills. Cameron joins the group and gets closer than ever to dunking but is not quite smooth enough to flip the ball down.

The boys become earnest, silent except for loud "aahs!"

as they jump into the night air. "Yeh, I hear you!" they shout to each other, sweating and tossing off their shirts. "In his face!"

There is an atmosphere of ritual surrounding the event, as though Cameron is in the company of braves, with Lloyd a chief watching from the perimeter. What I have seen of dunks in playground games has made me realize their importance: a man can leave his opponent behind with fancy dribbling or he can embarrass him by blocking his shot or stealing the ball, but nothing makes a statement of dominance better than a resounding stuff shot.

After one shot the ball bounces into the street and one of the players chases it, nearly getting run down by a bus. "That's the spirit Leon," they yell. When the player returns, Lloyd asks for the ball. He takes it and saunters to the front of the line. "You just not cool enough, Cameron," he says.

Carefully removing his shirt and folding it into a square which he places on the sidelines, Lloyd palms the ball and looks at the basket ten yards away. He puts the ball down and reaches into his pockets, pulling out an Afro pick, some change, and a dollar bill. He places these things on top of his neatly folded shirt and then picks up the ball. He rolls his shoulders two or three times and starts loping toward the basket. When he is close enough, his skinny legs uncoil and he sails into the air, cradling the ball in the crook of his elbow before casually smashing it through the hoop.

He slowly returns to the front of the line. A player hands him the ball again. This time Lloyd runs in a little faster. While in midair he waves the ball around his head like a bolo before dunking. Again, he returns.

On his third approach he cocks his arm like a pitcher in his windup and throws a strike straight through the rim at the pavement.

For his final attempt Lloyd walks back an extra ten paces and blows on his hands. He grasps the ball in front of him and takes an all-out sprint at the basket. He cuts sharply through the row of silent boys like a halfback turning upfield and then, nearly ten feet from the hoop, flings himself into the air. As he floats slowly to the rim he rubs the ball on the back of his neck like a man with an itch under his collar and then slams it through the rim so hard it caroms wildly off to another court.

Lloyd walks silently back to the sideline. He picks up his comb and change and puts them in his pocket. He picks up his shirt and puts it on, buttoning it as carefully as he removed it.

The lines start moving again, with added energy and a sense of respect. But Cameron has peaked and will not dunk tonight.

Ron Shelton

—

From White Men Can't Jump

Black Sidney (Wesley Snipes) and white Billy (Woody Harrelson) are driving home through L.A., having just won $5,000 in a Two-on-Two Basketball Tournament.

BILLY

I can jam.

SIDNEY

Good.

BILLY

I mean you keep telling everybody I can't stuff it.

SIDNEY

I was just trying to get under your skin.

BILLY

But I *can* dunk a basketball—just 'cause I don't in a game don't mean I can't.

SIDNEY

Fine . . .

BILLY

You don't think I can.

SIDNEY

I don't care if you can or can't.

BILLY

Stop the car.

SIDNEY PULLS THE CAR to the curb. By now they're on Washington Boulevard headed east.

SIDNEY

Okay.

BILLY

Turn that shit down.

SIDNEY SMILES and turns the music down.

SIDNEY

What?

BILLY

I'll bet your half of the five grand against my half of the five grand that I can jam.

Sidney stares at him like he's crazy. He is.

SIDNEY

(*calmly*)

Billy, listen to me. Go buy your girlfriend a nice dress in case she gets on that fucking game show,

and give the rest of the money to her for safe keeping.
(*beat*)
You're either stupid or dangerous and I know you aren't stupid 'cause you push my buttons and piss me off and stupid people can't do that.
(*beat*)
So you must be dangerous.

BILLY

To who?

SIDNEY

To yourself. Take the money and go home.

BILLY

You don't think I can stuff it.

SIDNEY

I'm taking you home.

SIDNEY PULLS BACK out into traffic. But Billy won't stop.

BILLY

The reason I don't stuff in a game is 'cause it's a waste of energy, it's showboating just for the sake of showboating, like a behind-the-back-pass when it's unnecessary—
(*relentless*)
It goes back to this thing I was saying—quoting myself—"A white man wants to win first, look good second. A black man wants to look good first, and win second—"

SIDNEY SLAMS ON THE BRAKES—The car screeches to a halt. Billy crashes into the dashboard ingloriously.

SIDNEY

That's enough. There's a hoop. Get your money and the ball.

P.O.V. A HOOP in an abandoned used car lot.

CUT TO:

EXT. THE USED CAR LOT HOOP—NIGHT

SIDNEY AND BILLY ARE ALL BUSINESS—This bet has nothing to do with anything but ego.

CLOSE ON THE TWO CHECKS—Each hand scribbles on the back.

SIDNEY

There. I've signed mine over to you and you sign yours over to me. Whoever wins gets both checks and can scratch out the sign-over. Okay, you done? Let's go.

BILLY STRETCHES TO GET LOOSE—He's stiffer than he thought.

SIDNEY (*cont'd*)

You stiff? Good, you oughta be.
Only played six games today.

BILLY

I can stuff in my sleep.

BILLY STRETCHES SERIOUSLY NOW—Picks up the basketball, spins it a few times, getting the feel again.

BILLY

Do I get a practice?

SIDNEY

Shit yeah, take all you want—you can practice all night—

BILLY

I don't want no fucking practice.
Three tries—all I need.

BILLY EYES THE BASKET—He's proven himself as such a quality athlete by now that we can't imagine he can't stuff—yet he's not that tall, 6 feet perhaps, and Sidney's right—he hasn't dunked in any games, so . . .

CLOSE ON SIDNEY—He's wondering the same things.

SIDNEY

One of us won't be going home tonight.

Billy eyes the hoop.

BILLY

You think that hoop's regulation?

SIDNEY

Let me check it out for you—

SIDNEY LEAPS EASILY UP TO GRAB THE RIM—He hangs for several beats, checking it out, taunting Billy with his easy jump. He drops back to the ground.

SIDNEY (*cont'd*)

Yeah . . . feels just about right to me . . .

BILLY DRIVES HARD TO THE HOOP—He skies with the ball—but he jams it into the front of the rim. It falls away harmlessly.

SIDNEY RETRIEVES THE BALL—Flips it to Billy. He is unbearably condescending.

SIDNEY (*cont'd*)

Good try, Billy, very good effort.
Let me pump you up a little.

SIDNEY REACHES DOWN TO "PUMP" air into Billy's shoes but, of course, they're not the right brand. He pumps anyway till Billy shoves him away.

BILLY

Get away from me . . . I almost had it.

BILLY IS DEEP IN CONCENTRATION this time. His nostrils flare, his breathing is quick and concentrated—

BILLY MOVES TO THE BASKET AGAIN—Explodes high, but—
THE BALL SLIPS OUT OF HIS HAND on the way up. He easily grabs the rim to steady himself, but—

SIDNEY

O for two. Y'know I thought the hoop was a little high at first too—it deceived me a little but it's just an optical illusion, I think . . .

BILLY

Fuck me. I had it . . .

BILLY GRABS THE BALL and with full focus of con-

centration he returns to his spot. It's obvious that he has the physical skills, though because of his height everything has to go perfectly—timing mostly.

CLOSE ON BILLY—The intensity of Karpov and Kasparov. This is it.

CLOSE ON SIDNEY—If he has doubts about the outcome it doesn't show in his manner. Cool as a cucumber.

SIDNEY

Billy . . .

BILLY

Shut up . . .

SIDNEY

Billy . . .

BILLY

Shut up . . .

SIDNEY

Billy . . .

BILLY

What?

SIDNEY

White men can't jump.

BILLY CHARGES TO THE HOOP—He leaps up, high, even high enough to slam, but—

THE BALL RICOCHETS OFF THE BACK RIM—Rebounding far away.

BILLY STANDS THERE FOOLISHLY—Feeling like an idiot.

BILLY
(*muttering to himself*)
I had it . . . I had it . . .

SIDNEY
You had this.

SIDNEY PICKS UP THE TWO *CHECKS—Holds them up.*

SIDNEY (*cont'd*)
Billy . . . you're a loser.

BILLY
I'm not a loser . . .
(*beat*)
. . . I'm just bad with money.

SIDNEY TURNS AND WALKS TO HIS CAR, laughing a little to himself at this simple explanation.

SIDNEY
Good luck with Gloria . . .

BILLY (*defiantly*)
I'm the best playground player in Los Angeles.

SIDNEY STOPS BEFORE ENTERING HIS CAR—Addresses Billy.

SIDNEY

You ain't even the best player in the Crenshaw District.

BILLY

Who's better?

SIDNEY

Me.

Pete Axthelm

"The Fallen Idol: The Harlem Tragedy of Earl Manigault" *From* The City Game

Faces light up as Harlem veterans reminisce about Manigault. Many street players won reputations with elaborate innovations and tricks. Jackie Jackson was among the first to warm up for games by picking quarters off the top of the backboard. Willie Hall, the former St. John's leader, apparently originated the custom of jumping to the top of the board and, instead of merely blocking a shot, slamming a hand with tremendous force against the board; the fixture would vibrate for several seconds after the blow, causing an easy lay-up to bounce crazily off the rim. Other noted leapers were famous for "pinning"—blocking a lay-up, then simply holding it momentarily against the backboard in a gesture of triumph. Some players seemed to hold it for seconds, suspended in air, multiplying the humiliation of the man who had tried the futile shot. Then they could slam the ball back down at the shooter or, for special emphasis, flip it into the crowd.

Earl Manigault did all those things and more, borrowing, innovating, and forming one of the most exciting styles Harlem crowds ever watched. Occasionally, he would drive past a few defenders, dunk the ball with one hand, catch it with the other—and raise it and stuff it through the hoop a second time before returning to earth.

"I was in the eighth grade when Earl was in the eleventh," said Charley Yelverton, now a star at Fordham. "I was just another young kid at the time. Like everybody else on the streets, I played some ball. But I just did it for something to do. I wasn't that excited about it. Then there happened to be a game around my block, down at 112th Street, and a lot of the top players were in it—and Earl came down to play. Well, I had never believed things like that could go on. I had never known what basketball could be like. Everybody in the game was doing something, stuffing or blocking shots or making great passes. There's only one game I've ever seen in my life to compare to it—the Knicks' last game against the Lakers.

"But among all the stars, there was no doubt who was the greatest. Passing, shooting, going up in the air, Earl just left everybody behind. No one could turn it on like he could."

Keith Edwards, who lived with Earl during the great days of the Young Life team, agreed. "I guess he had about the most natural ability that I've ever seen. Talent for talent, inch for inch, you'd have to put him on a par with Alcindor and the other superstars. To watch him was like poetry. To play with him or against him—just to be on the same court with him—was a deep experience.

"You can't really project him against an Alcindor, though, because you could never picture Earl going to UCLA or anyplace like that. He was never the type to really face his responsibilities and his future. He didn't want to think ahead. There was very little discipline about the man. . . ."

Ian O'Connor

"A King Felled by Drugs Revisits Court He Ruled"

"I am a rich man," Earl Manigault said. "Just look at my arms. All of my money is in my veins."

Manigault does not hesitate to show the track marks that race around his lean arms, the result of shooting heroin into his system for the better part of 13 years. He points to small circles around the tracks. "If you didn't hit the vein correctly, you'd get the swelling," he said. "We'd call them 'misses.' "

Last weekend, Manigault, the most gifted New York playground athlete never to make it to the National Basketball Association, came home. Manigault, who now lives on the brink of poverty in Charleston, S.C., returned to the park on 98th Street and Amsterdam Avenue where he was once so popular that in 1977 the local residents played a tournament named after him while he was in the Bronx House of Detention on weapons and drug charges.

What Manigault found was that nearly 25 years after he ruled the city's playgrounds, his legend remains intact.

Part of the Manigault mystique is that he never made it, that he succumbed to the street life that consumed many of his friends in the 1960's. The man Kareem Abdul Jabbar once called "the best basketball player his size in the history of New York City" became a drug addict and a thief, not an N.B.A. star.

"For every Michael Jordan, there's an Earl Manigault," Manigault said. "We all can't make it. Somebody has to fail. I was the one."

As the 44-year-old Manigault walks through the small park, only a few blocks from where he grew up, he is instantly recognized. Everyone he passes approaches Manigault (pronounced MAN-eh-galt) to offer greetings. Most of his friends and admirers call him the Goat, the nickname he picked up when a junior high school teacher kept pronouncing his name "Mani-Goat." Some just call him Legend.

Manigault hardly looks like a hero. At 6 feet 1 inch and 175 pounds, he is not a particularly big man. He moves through the park with a cigarette hanging from his mouth, carrying a can of beer in a brown paper bag and sipping through a straw. He is dressed in a faded T-shirt and blue shorts. He hunches slightly when he walks.

But while the neighborhood residents now see a shell of the athlete they once idolized, they also remember the pride he brought to them.

They remember his soaring dunks over much taller opponents that thrilled the audiences at the Rucker Tournament in Harlem. They remember his duels against the playground stars who made it, Connie Hawkins and Abdul-Jabbar (then Lew Alcindor), and those who did not, Joe Hammond and the late Herman (the Helicopter) Knowings, for example. They remember the time he dunked a ball backwards 36 times in a row to win a $60 bet.

"His ability to play like a man who was 6-9 was incredible," said Gene Williams, an organizer of the Rucker Tournament who played against Manigault in high school. "He was a phenomenal player. And he's still a legend to the kids today."

Manigault established a reputation as a remarkable leaper as a teen-ager, outplaying older, taller competitors. He starred at Benjamin Franklin High School until he was dismissed from school in his senior year for smoking marijuana in the locker room, a charge he denies. He then went to Laurinburg Institute, a North Carolina prep school, where he played for one year, finishing second-to-last in his class but taking home a high school degree.

The major college recruiters went after Manigault with zeal, as stories of his dunks and emphatic shot-blocking in the Harlem playgrounds at 129th Street and Seventh Avenue and at 155th Street and Eighth Avenue spread throughout the city. But Manigault feared that he couldn't handle the academic work at a prominent college, and he chose to attend Johnson C. Smith University, a predominantly black school in Charlotte, N.C. He struggled in the classroom, didn't get along with the coach and lasted less than a year.

With no thought of returning to college, Manigault realized basketball would take him no farther than the playgrounds. "That's when I went right to the bottom," he recalled. "I started messing with the 'white lady.' "

It wasn't long before Manigault had a heroin habit that cost more than $100 a day. He went to Manhattan's garment district to steal mink coats to support his addiction. Drug dealers would give him heroin for free, "because I was the Goat," he said, "and they didn't want to see me stealing for it."

The one thing that Manigault felt was untouchable, his basketball ability, soon deteriorated. He remembered a game in the 1965 Rucker Tournament when he lost his balance and fell twice, a shameful experience that steered him away from the game and toward the street corners, where he nodded pathetically, strung out in full view of the neighborhood.

Manigault was arrested for possession of drugs in 1969, the same year Abdul-Jabbar was made a rookie millionaire by the Milwaukee Bucks. He spent 18 days in the Tombs, where he fought urges to commit suicide and kicked his habit. He was then transferred to Green Haven prison in Stormville, N.Y., where he served 16 months of a five-year sentence.

In 1970, Manigault, at the age of 25, got his only shot at professional basketball. Bill Daniels, the owner of the Utah Stars of the American Basketball Association, read about Manigault in *The City Game* (Harper's Magazine Press, 1970), a book written by Pete Axthelm. Daniels gave Manigault a tryout, but the Legend had abused his body for too long.

"I drove Earl to the airport when he flew out to Utah," said Willie Mangham, one of Manigault's former teammates at Benjamin Franklin. "But it was too late for him. His body had been through too much. He couldn't take the pace."

Manigault said he stayed clean for several years. Ironically, he went to the drug kingpins for money to start his Goat Tournament, which was played at 98th and Amsterdam, then known as Goat Park. "I told them they had to give something back to the community," Manigault said. "They couldn't say no to the Goat."

But the Goat couldn't say no to drugs. He started dabbling in heroin again. On a rainy summer day in 1977, the first day of the Goat Tournament was canceled and Manigault got into a car with some friends and headed to the Bronx. "We had a plan to steal $6 million," said Manigault, who refuses to reveal the plan. "But we got busted. They figured I was the ringleader. I got two years."

After two years in the Bronx House of Detention and the state prison in Ossining, Manigault took two of his sons, the youngest of his seven children (he never married), and moved to Charleston to get out of the city and away from the lure of drugs. "I didn't want my sons to be greater junkies than I was," he said.

Manigault says he hasn't touched drugs since he left the city. He lives with his two sons in a small home in Charleston, and has survived by painting houses, mowing lawns and working for the local recreation department. He has never held a full-time job for any length of time.

The playground at 98th and Amsterdam is still called Goat Park by the neighborhood, although a sign on the chain fence now declares it "The Happy Warrior Playground." When Manigault is in town, word spreads and people head for the park. They come to wish him well, to buy him a beer or a pack of cigarettes.

Manigault's hold on the people is not restricted to the

poor or to blacks. Stephen F. Cohen, the director of the Russian studies program at Princeton University and the author of numerous books on Soviet history and politics, is proof.

Cohen, a self-proclaimed "basketball junkie" and a former neighborhood resident, met Manigault in the late 1960's and they have been close friends since. Cohen said he was touched by the genuine sweetness of Manigault, and by the way he'd smile to the children or tell a joke to an admirer.

"Earl has absolutely no meanness in him," Cohen said. "If Earl ever did anything to anybody, he did it to himself. That's the tragedy."

Manigault's personality is one of the reasons the neighborhood people still treat him with reverence. Despite all his failures, he is still regarded as a king of sorts, a ruler of the two blocks that connect Goat Park to Frederick Douglass Playground on 100th Street.

"Earl lived like exiled royalty on these mean streets," Cohen said. "He lived on the kindness of admirers. He had job opportunities, but he'd always walk away from them because he never had to worry about anything."

Today, Manigault worries about his health. Two heart operations, including corrective surgery on two valves last February, left him with huge scars and took away any stamina he had left. He still shows flashes of his brilliance in pickup games, but he cannot sustain a consistent pace for more than five minutes. When asked if he could still dunk a basketball, Manigault smiled but didn't answer.

After shooting baskets for 15 minutes, Manigault rests on a bench in his park and rubs his muscular legs. He is proud of his legs, the springs that once carried him over the other playground stars. The most striking aspect of his legs is that there are no tracks or "misses" to be found on them.

"When the veins in my arms were full, it was tempting to go to my legs," Manigault said. "But I've always loved my legs. No matter how bad it got, I always went to another spot on my arms."

When everyone in the park has had the chance to see Manigault, it is time for the Goat to head uptown. As he leaves the park, a man on the corner stops him and offers a beer. The exiled king in the faded T-shirt, the ex-junkie and convict, has received another gift.

"I let thousands of people down," Manigault said. "But I'm nothing phony. And there was a time when I gave the people what they wanted."

David O. Weber

American Pastime

The College Football Game of the Week was flickering into its fourth desultory quarter. The score was tied 0–0. There was time out on the field for an injury.

I was bored. I stretched my legs and yawned. I hooked my desert boots over the arm of a couch.

"Watch it," the guy on the couch snarled. He knocked my feet off the wicker with his elbow.

"Screw you," I muttered. Pro forma. I adjusted myself in my seat.

The camera zoomed in on the injured player. He was lying motionless, supine. Clipped chasing a four-yard punt return. A couple of his teammates stood over him—impassive, hands on hips, studying the cheerleaders. A trainer dashed up and unfastened the man's helmet straps. The camera dollied in closer so we could see his pain.

A jet whined overhead. Low, coming in for a landing. The picture began to flipflop.

"Shit. Fix it," people grunted.

Somebody reached across and fiddled with the vertical hold. The network cut away for a commercial.

I got up. I left the lounge, took the elevator up to my room, and changed my clothes. Watching all that physical performance had excited me. I put on an old sweatshirt and hurriedly laced my basketball shoes. With luck there might be two hours of good light left. I drank some water from the faucet in the corner basin. I glanced at the books on my desk. My thesis outline is almost finished. It is excruciatingly dull. I dug my ball out of the bottom of the closet and took the elevator to street level.

The weather outside was gunmetal. Dead as the season, drained, even, of season. The temperature was about fifty. The air was heavy, and its humidity seemed to have soaked into the garbage and the puffy scraps of newspaper that lay heavily in the gutters. Occasionally a gust of wind—chill and dry and stale as a smoker's cough—ruffled the litter. The sky was thick with meaningless clouds. Sky and building stones leached the same empty gray. Rain was unlikely, sun was unthinkable, and snow was impossible.

I spun my basketball on my finger, let it wobble, fall off. I dribbled it on the pavement. At this dead hour of a Saturday afternoon, the street was nearly deserted. The thoing-thoing-thoing as the hard rubber sphere met the sidewalk echoed and reverberated off the high-rise building fronts. The noise startled me. It seemed an impolite intrusion into the quiet lives sequestered behind these blind windows. A cab cruised by. The driver watched me sleepily. A dark-bearded professorial type with an armload of groceries shot me a disapproving eye as he ducked into his apartment entryway. I almost dribbled on a smear of dogshit. I tucked the ball over my hip.

The university is three blocks north. At South Campus Drive the view suddenly opens out. You can see across the pinched quadrangle and the cupolaed administration building, through the crane-topped skeletons of a distant construction project, to the flight-space over tri-county airport. Behind the library there are gnarled maples. Arms bleak and bare in winter, but vegetable. Unhealthy grass hibernates in the quadrangle. Still, whenever I round this corner, I experience a lift—a momentary unclenching of my ribs, a respite from the claustrophobia I recognize now only by its absence. I remember the great stretch of continent around me—and alternatives . . . adventures, even . . . seem once more possible.

Two coeds passed, carrying their breasts on their books.

A block west the architecture closes in again. Just a little farther down, the housing projects start. But here it's still university property. The court is wedged behind a pair of massive buildings—laboratories, I think. All the windows, all the way up, have heavy mesh guards. This used to be a truck-loading bay. You can see the bricked-up outline along one enclosing wall where the dock was. Now there's an asphalt surface with a set of white lines, and a couple of flimsy backboards on metal poles, and a high chain-link fence with a gate and a padlock. Empty soft-drink cans and moldering slivers of orange peel collect in the corners. The asphalt wears a fine layer of grit sifted out of the sky. The only entrance is by a short defile—once a driveway—between the buildings. There's a gate outside there too, and a sign warning, "This facility restricted to use by students, faculty, and employees of . . ."

The university's name has been obliterated by obscenities and initialed love pledges.

Since the troubles last spring, official policy has been to open all recreational areas to the wider community. Apparently no one has yet thought to take down that sign.

When I arrived, I found I had the court to myself. I dribbled to the near basket and hoisted a right-hand lay-up. It circled the rim and flipped out. It's only very recently that I have taken up the game again. There wasn't a great deal of opportunity in the Mekong Delta.

For a while I just stayed in close to the basket, practicing bunnies and tip-ins. Loosening up while I got the feel of the boards. The rims at both ends of the court were slightly askew—hung on too many times by aspiring Alcindors. There were brand-new string nets, though. They'd get slashed or stolen before long, so I figured I'd better enjoy them while I could. A net changes the action off the rim, and offers a better target for the shooter's eye. The ball settles in more satisfyingly, too, somehow—nestles for an instant before dropping.

I backed off about eight feet to the left and arched a high bank shot. Missed. I raced after the ball, dribbled twice, leaped, and fired for the board. Banked—in. Still, it would take me a few shots to get the angles down really pat. In college that had been my most consistent weapon. I played forward—small, at six-two, but faky. I once scored twenty-four points in a game. Twenty, as I recall, on banked jumpers from the left. One of those unconscious radar nights when all you've got to do to score, it seems, is loft the ball in the vaguest general direction of the backboard.

I worked my way around the key, recalling past glories.

I went to a tiny, expensive liberal-arts college whose teams competed, lackadaisically, in a tiny, patrician conference. There weren't many glories.

I was beginning to breathe hard. I slowed down. I moved over to the foul line. In high school I shot fouls with two hands, in college with one. Now I favor a jump shot. I wanted to test its effectiveness.

I had put together a string of six when another guy came. A spade. He sauntered down the driveway toward the court. He was wearing a short tan windbreaker, a pair of dressy-looking tight gold trousers, and blue canvas track shoes—the kind with three diagonal white stripes along the insteps. He had a natural haircut—not too high, but full enough for militancy. Hard to tell if he was from the university or the ghetto. He moved with that pained Negro nonchalance—torso slowly twisting, arms dangling loose behind his buttocks, wrists cocked, head back, rising and rocking with each step on the balls of his feet. He paused at the out-of-bounds line to watch me shoot. I felt a challenge, a slight nervousness. I spun the ball under my splayed fingertips, gave it a bounce, stepped lightly to my left, jumped, and shot. Arching the ball high from behind my head for a swish.

Swish.

I went to retrieve the ball. Nodding, deadpan, faintly, along the way. He met my eye and nodded back. I spun in a little left-handed bunny, using English. He had taken a step forward onto the court. As the ball fell through the net, I batted it to him. He picked up the pass, made a head feint, leaped straight into the air, tucked his heels under his rump, and fired a swish.

I was impressed.

We shot together for a while, silent. Competing in a way, judging each other, but never acknowledging it. The guy was good. We'd take turns, one under the basket feeding the other, exchanging places on a miss. Or, in his case, when he'd completed an outside circuit. I always have one or two spots where, beyond fifteen feet, I'm inconsistent. Still, I was hitting pretty well. I used my body very deliberately, always unwinding at half-speed, as though stiff and sore. But never jerky. Making a point of ease. With the spade it was natural—they almost always have a better body sense than whites. And more basketball skill. But there was, between us, a mutuality of competence. At least, I thought so. It manifested itself in the slightly detached, leisurely way in which we both moved and shot. And took each basket for granted. Flashing inward, ironic half-smiles when a shot—occasionally—rimmed the target.

We'd been going for about ten minutes, maybe, when a third guy showed up. He brought his own ball. We could hear him coming by the sound of its bounce. I winced. The spade gave me a fast, flickering look—a hesitant, unguarded sharing of opinion. The noise that ball made was itself an affront to the sport. Like an inflated hot-water bottle, or the sort of soft yellow toy one sees floating in suburban wading pools. We both became very intent on our shooting.

The guy turned out, as we had feared, to match his ball. Short pudgy legs and breasts that jiggled. Hips. A sparse black beard—square, Mosiac—framing a fleshy face. Somehow the beard made it look even more juvenile. He wore a powder blue sweatshirt and matching Keds. The sweatshirt said CORNELL.

He dribbled onto the court, poking at the ball intently

until he was at a forty-five-degree angle to the basket, then caught it and smiled at us.

"Hi," he said. "Mind if I shoot with you cats?"

My black companion made no response. He was busy preparing to sink a twenty-foot turn-around fall-away jump.

I shrugged. "Help yourself," I muttered.

He nodded. He gave his ball an inexpert bounce, clasped his tongue between his molars, and suddenly, with an awkward lunge, pushed off a shot. He fired it one-handed, stiff-armed, as though it were too heavy for him. The motion was like a girl's. Or a little kid's—the way I used to shoot when I was in grammar school. The ball's trajectory was much too hard and flat for that distance. It struck the backboard and rim simultaneously, still on the rise. It wedged itself firmly between the two.

"Great beginning." The guy chuckled. As though things would improve. "Huh?" He wagged his head, trotted in under the basket, and to my astonishment, made a futile, lumbering little leap at the ball. It was ridiculous—he couldn't have been more than five-feet-seven.

He put his shoulder against the pole and began to shake it.

"Hey," I said, my voice, I hoped, trickling disapproval. "Here. Watch it." I loped to the basket, sprang, and smashed the ball loose.

"You've got a good jump there, man," he told me. He waddled off in pursuit of his ball.

The spade had gone to the other end of the court. I couldn't blame him—the backboard here was still vibrating. I watched him take a couple of graceful shots. I leaned against the oscillating iron pole to steady it. The new guy popped away around me. His form wasn't getting any better, but he actually started to sink some baskets. If the ball fell within arm's reach, I'd tap it back to him. He made one from the right corner. I fed him and he made a second. Amazing. On the third try he missed the hoop entirely. I snagged the ball in flight and came out from under the basket to have a shot myself. But dribbling it was like bouncing an inner tube. The ball was too smooth and too light and too resilient, and not quite the right size, and even the wrong color. An embarrassing carroty orange. It wasn't, I decided now, worth the dignity of a real shot. I flicked it up carelessly with my wrist. It struck the front of the rim, *sproïng,* and bounded high over the top of the board.

I had already turned away to stare at the spade. I was growing a little annoyed. He showed no signs of coming back. There he was, blithely firing away with my ball—my good ball—all by himself. It put me in a minor quandary. If I went to join him, it would seem a rather obvious slight to the newcomer. Why I should have cared, I didn't know. Still . . . On the other hand, he was, after all, using my equipment. I stood there with my hand on my hip. Waiting to see if the message would spark across the distance.

It didn't.

After a minute I cleared my throat. "Hey, man," I called. The first words I had spoken to him. "You going to keep that ball down there all day?" I added a friendly smile.

He looked at me, expressionless, then turned his back. He uncoiled languorously into the air, hung for a long instant—drawing it out purposefully, haughtily—before bucketing a bullet. He retrieved the ball and dribbled slowly up the asphalt toward me. When he got within range, he passed it—snappy, level, and chest-high. A textbook pass. It stung my palms. I cocked him a thanks, but his eyes had wandered. He plunged his hands into his jacket pockets—I just then realized he had never even warmed up enough to take it off—and strolled toward the street. He had resumed that peculiar black swagger. Elbows pinched back like folded wings, mincing in a way that was both masculine and menacing. I took a shot before I realized he was actually leaving. I was surprised. My immediate instinct was to apologize. I felt that I was at fault somehow. I was disappointed, too. The prospect of being left alone with this other scuttling clown was a distinct gloomer. It was his maladroit intrusion that had broken up our cool communion. I almost said something—urged the spade to stick around. But I knew it would only be an unproductive lapse in my own dignity.

"Say," piped up Cornell, "how about a little two-on-one? Anybody interested?"

The earnestness with which he peered into our faces was amusing. It was an absurd suggestion—but I waited to see what the spade's reaction would be. He didn't even break step. He made only the barest negative moue with his thick lips.

Just then three guys wearing gym suits wheeled around the corner. Laughing and jostling one another, obviously ready for exercise. The one in the middle cradled a leather basketball. "University Gym #22" was inked prominently between the seams. They bustled down the driveway toward us, split apart to flow around the spade, converged again, and suddenly broke into a weaving, shouting, passing pattern. They dashed noisily past us and whooped to the other end of the court. Everything about them gave off energy. It was a little dumbfounding. In a second they were back, firing at our backboard and playfully zipping tricky passes between their legs and behind their backs. The guy who had carried the ball stepped aside toward me.

"Well, what are we waiting for?" He grinned. "Let's get started. It'll be dark before long. How about it? You guys accept the challenge? Or you want to shoot for sides?"

I laughed, though I was a bit dubious at his gusto. I scuffed a toe along the out-of-bounds line. "Fine with me," I said. I glanced over at the spade. "Only, I'm not sure there's enough. He was just leaving."

"Yeah?" The trio leader turned to confront him. "What about it? Little three-on-three? Come on." He beckoned jovially with his head. "Couple of games, okay?"

The spade had halted to observe the flurry. He stood impassive for a second. Then shrugged.

"Great! I'm Dick. That's Doug . . . and Phil, with the ball."

He thrust out his hand.

"Dave," I grunted. He gave my knuckles a Kiwanis squeeze.

He strode to the spade. "Dick," he repeated, hand out. The spade accorded it a limp tap. I couldn't hear the name he mumbled.

Cornell, who was doggedly practicing his 1937 one-handed set shots while the other two frisked around him, got the treatment next. "Morton," he blinked in reply.

Dick turned to me. "How about if we three stand you guys?" As he spoke, he calmly lifted Cornell's—Morton's—ball out of his hands and gave it a tentative bounce. "Crappy," he adjudged. He drop-kicked it into a far corner.

The spade and I looked at each other. Silently weighing

the handicap Morton would present. Finally I made a face. "Why not?"

"We can always," Dick added, "change things around later. At least this way the height's fairly evened out."

The spade was over by the gate, removing his jacket. He wore a dark blue T-shirt. His legs were long and skinny, calfless, but he had well-developed buttocks. The thigh-tight gold pants emphasized them. In fact, he was very slender—but now I could see that his shoulders and upper arms were smoothly muscled. He was probably an inch or so shorter than I am. The wooly bubble of hair made him look taller.

"Let's see that ball," Dick commanded. He gestured at me.

I tossed it to him underhand. "It's best," I said firmly.

He accepted my simple declarative. He dribbled it a couple of times. "Okay. Do-or-die?"

Since the spade wasn't talking much, I answered. "Be my guest."

He was already far enough back, nearly at midcourt line. He lofted a high soft push shot, going up off his toes. The ball plummeted cleanly through the net. Hm. Their out, then. Half-court, winners keep, have to take the ball back beyond the foul line on exchange of hands. Unless it misses both backboard and rim. Play to twenty-four points. We agreed on the rules.

It occurred to me, from that shot, that we might be overmatched.

But, as it turned out, it was never really a contest. We assigned Morton to Doug, who was about the same height—crew-cut and red-faced, and a little too burly to be fast. He had probably played second-string guard on his high-school football team. The spade covered Dick, and I took Phil, their big man. On the first inbound play, Dick began a fancy drive for the basket. The spade effortlessly, almost apologetically, stole the ball. He spun to his left. Dick was still lamely paddling air. Phil had dropped off behind me to clear the lane. I was alone. The spade flicked a pass at my midsection. I grabbed it, took a step backward, went up twisting to my right. The ball banked smoothly into the hoop just as Phil recovered and clobbered me.

We scored eight straight baskets after that. Finally I made the generous mistake of feeding Morton. Even so, we won 24–8.

"Okay, you guys were lucky," Dick panted. "How about another? You can't stay that hot all day."

So we started a second game. The spade inbounded the ball to Morton, who worked his way down the right sideline. Doug hounded him violently—windmilling his arms, stamping his feet, bellying up close, and bumping with a ferocity that owed more to football line play than aggressive basketball defense. Morton almost lost the ball about six times. I kept dancing around them, yelling for a pass. Trying to rescue him. But Morton floundered grittily on. At the last moment, driven deep into the corner and virtually toppling out of bounds, he looped up a shot. It was blind, desperate, off the wrong foot, and badly forced. It rippled through the basket without even brushing the rim.

Then the spade scored on a twisting, leaping hook—an absolutely indefensible move. Dick, it had become clear, was a good athlete. Agile, quick to react, hard to fake off-balance. But he was giving away a couple of precious inches. The spade could go over him anytime he really wanted to. Besides, the spade had incredible timing. The ball, when he maneuvered, was like a growth on his palm. No matter how dexterously Dick slapped at it, it always seemed to be protected. Out of reach, nestled safe in the warm butterscotch lee of those chocolate fingers. He would start with the ball well in front of his body. Bouncing it high, taunting Dick to commit himself. Then suddenly he would lunge, whirl, stop and go, stop, shift, crouch, launch a shoulder in one direction, pull back, peel off in the other, feint, surge into the air, and—with a soft, deft flutter of wrists and fingertips—sail the ball on a gentle parabolic path to the core of the basket. He was beautiful to watch—especially when he was on your side.

Then it was my turn. I had been matching him practically shot for shot, even though I was at something of a disadvantage. Like Dick, I was giving away height to my man. Phil was maybe six-four or -five, and he outweighed me by a good thirty pounds. That meant he should have been able to screen me out pretty effectively under the basket. Only thing was, we weren't missing. So rebounds didn't make any difference. Then, too, I was more nimble than Phil. Normally I dislike playing in the center, where everybody bunches up and disembodied arms flail and giant paws abruptly loom to pluck the ball out of your hands or pound it back down into your face. I would prefer to range along the fringes of the court. Like the spade, one-on-one, using cuts and guile to make my openings. But between the uncanny passing of my black teammate and my own cute footwork, I was enjoying astonishing success. Everything I tried dropped—hooks, short fall-away jumpers, sneaky underhand caroms off the board . . . even a tip-in I managed to worm around Phil for. I was cocky and loose. The spade cruised by the top of the key. He blasted a pass in at me. I speared it, looked left, dribbled twice;

leaned a hip into Phil, and immediately jerked away, uncoiling to shoot. I had him by a micro-second, but he vaulted high. The ball barely squeaked above his straining fingers . . . caught the side of the rim . . . rattled through.

I whirled, still on the tail of my momentum. I poked a conspiratory hand at the spade.

He slapped my palm.

Maybe I was still preoccupied with that gesture on the next play. It was the first time I had ever been given skin. Of course, I see it all the time on television these days. But I had never been on a team with a black. I felt, now, like an honorary spade. I grinned to myself. Actually, it had been a bit awkward. My fingers were slightly cupped, expecting a clasp. . . . But anyway, next play I set a pick for my soul brother. He drove around me and brushed off Dick. Phil came out to cover him. I released backward, and the spade fed me neatly. It was an easy lay-up, but I banked it too hard and Phil grabbed the rebound.

From there on, things tightened up. Dick scored on a couple of outside shots. The spade nodded good-naturedly. Phil started using his height better. There wasn't much I could do. I tried to harass him—keep a hand waving in his face, probe for the ball, jostle and hack when he went up above me for a shot. I didn't mean to foul him—strove not to—but I felt justified in working him over a bit roughly since he was so much bigger. There was no one around to call fouls anyway. Except the offender whose conscience smote him, or the offended who considered he had been egregiously mauled. It was just a casual game, though, so there was no reason to play too hard. I blocked as cleanly as I could. The score seesawed. Two more guys had wandered into the court—

spades. One was pretty tall. I saw them from the corner of my eye, watching us for a while. Then they went down to the other basket and shot.

At 16–all I pulled a misfire by Doug off the board. We worked it around and the spade hit a jumper. We had been allowing Morton his fair share of ball-handling, but he had gunned only once—and missed—since his opening two points. Now he got a chance, pumped from the same right corner and made it again. 20–16. The spade threw the ball inbounds to me. His moves were usually lazy, liquid. This time he darted for the basket. He was ahead of Dick, and I led him accurately. The ball hung . . . he bounded and tapped it in. 22–16. We had matters well in hand when we wanted.

The spade bounced off the chain-link fence behind the pole and circled out toward me with both hands extended. Faded palms flat, upturned. I smacked them with my own two palms. Pat-a-cake, the way I'd watched it on the tube. I hoped my style was sufficiently soulful.

So now we needed only one final basket. I took the inbound pass from Morton and headed for a good spot. Phil picked me up tight. I passed off to the spade and retreated underneath. The spade was well-covered. He gave the ball to Morton. Morton, like most mediocre players, had a tendency to hold the ball too long. And, under the kind of pressure Doug exerted, to get flustered. Which is exactly what he did. He hesitated—and Doug's arms snaked in to trap the ball against his paunch. The two of them grappled. The ball trickled loose. Dick and the spade lunged for it. The spade won. He scooped me a low pass. I thought I was free. I came up with it, twisting for the basket.

Instead I met Phil's elbow—square in the nose.

The world evaporated, returned at the edges. I was on my back on the asphalt. I had no sensation of falling—just of being in the air one moment and on the ground the next. There was a numb, ragged void in the center of my face. Quickly flooding with pain. I felt the bridge of my nose. Nothing seemed to be broken.

Everyone had clustered around me. I reached up a hand. Phil seized it and helped me haul myself to my feet.

"Jesus, I'm sorry," he said.

"Yeah. That's okay." I gave the beak another wiggle. Just to make sure. The part throbbed, but its substructure seemed all of a piece. Suddenly a long red stain materialized down the front of my sweatshirt.

"You got a nosebleed," somebody pointed out.

"Mm. Hm!" I licked my upper lip and tasted the salty fluid. Another drop splashed on my sweatshirt. I sniffled. I had to swallow as the back of my throat filled.

"Tilt your head, man."

"There ought to be some cold water around here or something."

"Breathe through your mouth."

"I'll be okay," I said. Bunch of experts. I arched my spine and craned backward, staring at the sky. I snuffled gently to clear the passage, inhaled through my nostrils, and pressed the side of my finger firmly into the base of the cartilage. It brought tears to my eyes.

The spade had recovered the ball. He dribbled it absently.

I'm not much of a bleeder. The wound clotted quickly. I didn't want to interrupt the game for long anyway. I spat.

Pink. I wiped my lip and mouth and chin on the sleeve of my sweatshirt.

"I think I'll claim a foul on that one," I said. I beckoned for the ball.

Phil nodded. There was no argument. If nothing else, my gore-smeared front had them cowed.

I took the ball out, passed it to the spade, who passed it back to me. Phil was a good five feet off, still atoning for his sins. He was inviting me to have a makeup shot as long as it was from the outside. So I popped. The ball was dead on the button. So we won, 24–16.

The other two spades had gravitated toward our game. As it ended, the shorter called out to my teammate, " 'Say, brother?"

He nodded familiarly and sauntered their way. The three of them stood at midcourt, bantering in high-pitched monosyllables. I went over by the fence and sat down for a moment. I was beginning to feel the effects of the exercise in my knee joints and calves and rib cage. My nose ached vaguely. I caressed it—sort of patted it into shape with the balls of my fingers, like a sculptor smoothing clay. There was still a spot at the crest where a touch made me wince. I rubbed my upper lip. Dried brown flakes crumbled away on my knuckle.

"You all right?" Phil stood spraddle-legged above me, his fair prairie face furrowed into a frown of concern. His sweat-grayed socks and shorts and T-shirt gave off sour locker odors. For some reason, I figured he was a law student.

"Yeah, fine," I said. "Really. No big deal."

"Great." He leaned down and clapped me on the shoulder. Then he wandered away.

Morton came up. He squatted beside me. He launched into a complex analysis of the game we had just played—where our mistakes lay, how we could have improved our offense and defense. You'd think we were the Boston Celtics. And he was Red Auerbach. I nodded politely where unavoidable.

"How about let's getting started again," Dick announced. "You guys ready?"

The taller spade stepped forward. "Hey, we got winners here, man."

"You never called it," Dick said.

"I call it now." He scowled.

"I already asked *him,* before," the short spade added. He jerked a thumb at my black teammate. "Didn't I, brother?"

The spade bobbed his head in slow agreement. Smiling a detached, belying smile.

"You've only got two," Dick objected.

"We'll pick one from the losers." The short guy grinned. He had a wispy goatee and mustache—their very patchiness somehow alien and evil. "We'll pick him." He pointed at Phil.

I pushed myself up from the asphalt. "Unh-unh. That's no good," I said. "The height's unfair."

The short spade stared at me for a second, then shrugged. "I don't give a shit, then, man. Let 'em shoot for it." He dribbled number twenty-two impatiently.

I had no desire to exert the efforts required to defend against two taller men. I offered a counter-proposal. "Why don't we play four-on-four instead? That way nobody has to sit out."

The short spade shook his head disgustedly. "Too crowded," he snapped.

But after a little more argument we reached a compromise. Everybody would play, four-on-four, new sides, we would shoot for sides. Dick went to the foul line first. He made his shot. Then the short spade ambled up. Damn, I thought, they all move with that same twitching grace. Atavistic instincts rippling through those supple frames. Hunters and veld runners itching to break loose, trapped in bodies condemned to the slack routines of civilization. Anyway, though, he missed. He chuckled. Doug and Phil both made their shots. Morton, after priming himself with great deliberation, missed. Too bad. I would have liked to play with the spades. Probably not the fairest division of talents, though.

The tall spade came forward. He was unusually skinny—all hands and knees and feet and elbow blades. His head seemed small, comparatively, for the rest of his body. Maybe because the hair was cropped close to the scalp, part and hairline artificially defined by a razor. He was quite young, I decided. Maybe even still in high school. I find it hard to read spade ages. I glanced at the guy I had been teamed with. He might have been much younger than I had originally thought, too. All three of the Negroes carried themselves with assurance—a sort of subtle abrasiveness—that contrasted with the unfocused callowness of the whites on the court. And yet the latter were probably all older. It was strange—the whites had tight bodies and loose-fitting characters. The blacks had taut, tailored characters and loose bodies. Or maybe it was just that the whites had control over neither, while the blacks were in full control of both. Even the gangling teenage spade—who walked with a stiltlike, bent-at-the-knees syncopation, like one who has not yet come fully to terms with his height—nevertheless had a natural self-possession. He was awkward the way a heron or a crane is awkward. He wagged his head at his companion and winked, as though there were some private joke involved. Then he shot and missed. A good thing—I would have howled again if he and Phil were together. He chuckled. He had looked to be trying. Still, I felt a glimmer of suspicion.

Only my spade ex-teammate and I were left. I hung back, giving him the initiative. He hesitated too.

"Go ahead," I said, with a courtesy wave at the line.

He dribbled forward and shot. The ball skidded around the hoop . . . oozed out. One of his few misses of the day.

I stepped up. I was tempted to aim off-target. I had hoped at last to team with *him* once more. But . . . what the hell. Let fate and my own skill decide. I jumped and flicked off my shot.

Swish.

So the sides were set. Dick and Doug and Phil and I against the three spades and Morton. Dick went through his handshake bit. The tall cat said his name was C.J. The short guy leered. "Pierre."

We put Dick on him. Phil, naturally, took C.J. Doug stayed with Morton. I volunteered to guard the first spade, whose name, apparently, I would never find out. C.J. knelt to tighten the grubby laces on his outsize black canvas high-tops. While we waited for the game to begin, I experienced a sudden adrenal tingle. That's pretty unusual for a pickup contest. Jitters. Something that comes with real competition—when you trot out, shaky, on the hardwood, varnish brittly reflecting the glare and the growl of the crowd. Well, working against the spade was going to present an interesting challenge.

And, almost as soon as we were into it, the game revealed itself as a beauty. I've played in sloppier intercollegiate contests. With only a couple of exceptions—Morton and, to a somewhat lesser extent, Doug—everyone of us was a capable, solid basketball player. There was a certain lack of organization, of course, but even that very quickly diminished as we picked up on one another's moves. At first, things were individualistic—few passes, the man with the ball finding his own openings to shoot. Accuracy excuses long-rangerism, though, and hands were definitely hot. First Dick scored, then Phil dropped a hook, then I spotted Doug breaking for the pole and laid a pass on him for two. Then Dick tried a jumper that was partially deflected. The spades came down with the ball. The short guy, Pierre, drove on Dick and edged around him. Next play Pierre sank an outside one-hander behind C.J.'s screen. Then it was Pierre again. His bank shot came off the rim, but the tall guy had position on Phil. He stuffed the rebound.

Six–all. My man had not yet handled the ball. He tossed in to Morton. Morton was tied up at once. Pierre pried the ball out of Doug's grasp, though, and set about trying to ditch Dick. Dick hung on—literally, his left hand thrust into the folds of Pierre's dangling shirttail. Finally Pierre reached around and slapped Dick's arm away. At the same instant, he whirled. He spun up an arching shot, but Dick was with him inch for inch. He got three fingers on the ball—but somehow it was not enough. The ball slopped through the hoop. Eight–six theirs. Pierre was a gunner. He was also a lucky son-of-a-bitch.

Now the spade was beginning to look disgruntled. Nine shots in the game, seven of them good, and he hadn't even touched the ball inbounds. He let Morton take it out. Morton passed to Pierre. Another one-man exhibition seemed about to unfurl. My man lounged sourly in the backcourt. Rooted in gloom. I glanced over to see if I could help out Dick on defense. First mistake. When I turned back, the spade had disappeared. There he was, damn it! Free in the corner. Pierre drilled a pass. The spade sank his shot easily.

I had been so thoroughly outwitted that time there was nothing I could do but watch. Hell. Just have to make sure that false languor didn't lull me again.

Next play it was Morton's turn to pull the unexpected. The little bastard threaded a perfect towering pass over Phil's defensive stretch. C.J. arrowed high, engulfed the ball in the prehensile digits of one hand, rotated in air, and rifled it savagely through the hoop, straight down. Superlative.

Pierre tossed the ball inbounds to my man. I played him close. He wasn't going to get me this time. I kept my weight evenly distributed, poised on the balls of my feet, ankles wide, curled body riding smoothly on knees that were cocked and limber. I tried to sense his moves in advance with my lee hand. Fingertips splayed against the bunched sinews at the pit of his back. He was sweating now, and his cotton T-shirt was wet through. He gave off a musky scent. He bobbed and stutter-stepped, testing me. I have quick reflexes, though—and long arms. I darted a hand around his hip. I batted the ball away, out of bounds.

So we were even. He wasn't invulnerable.

He threw the ball in to Pierre. Pierre took a shot and missed. Phil hauled down the rebound. He cleared the ball out to me. I worked it to Dick, Dick found Doug, Doug hit. Even the more inept among us were playing high.

I had a chance next. From the post, Phil caught me breaking away from the spade. A spin and feint . . . the pass was good and I went up for an unmolested jumper. The ball struck the inside back rim and bounced out. Crap.

C.J. fielded it. He cleared it to the spade. I took up where I had left off, determined to close him out. He stuck his rump into me and bulled toward the basket. He was sidling to my right. I thought I saw another opportunity for a steal. Worth a gamble, anyway. I lunged around him with my right hand. Second mistake. He had baited me into that one. He twirled off to the left, driving hard for the basket. My only hope was to tick the ball from behind. I swatted at it, missed. All I could do now was give chase. But suddenly, unexpectedly, he halted. I leaped desperately above him—sailing across his field of fire in a last-ditch attempt to block the shot. Phil too had unwound to defend. We collided heavily in midair. The spade just waited, lip curled, for the shock wave to subside. Then he hopped over us and banked a bunny.

"Son-of-a-bitch!" I moaned. I was disgusted with myself for having been tricked. Worse, Phil's shoulder had clipped my nose again. It was a glancing blow, softened by flesh. But it served to remind the cringing nerves of their recent insult. Phil dusted himself off. I walked around in jerky circles. Head bowed, nose cupped, muttering curses as I tried to restrain the pain. I felt a light tingle on my upper lip. Uh-oh. I examined my palm. Yep, I was bleeding again.

Phil had joined me. He draped a meaty, compassionate arm around my shoulders. His acrid stench seemed styptic—but wasn't. He leaned close and peered into my face. When he spotted the blood he stiffened. "Hey, time out, you guys," he called. His voice, I thought, had an exultant ring.

I shook him off angrily and threw back my head. "No, goddamnit!" I roared. "Come on! Let's go! Keep playing!"

My words were thick and bubbly. I sniffed hard. I strode to the spade and gave him a pat on the ass. A warm manly tribute—vanquished saluting the victor. I noticed, to my chagrin, a faint maroon smudge on the gold pants fabric where my hand had landed. I blinked away with a lurch of conscience. I gazed at the sky. I concentrated on willing my blood vessels to constrict. "Goddamnit!" I shouted. "Play!"

And so we did. The bleeding was only a trickle. It didn't hamper me that much. I gulped air through my mouth and occasionally daubed at my nostrils with the hem of my sweatshirt. Every so often a dark bead would flip off the end of my nose as I made a sudden movement. Pretty soon a couple of the others wore random splashes of my lurid sap. But nobody seemed to notice in the heat of the game. Anyway, there were other little wounds in the crowd too. Welling scrapes where a fingernail had raked, rasped skin where a knee or elbow had kissed asphalt. When I climb into the shower after a game, I always find myself disfigured with gouges and bruises I can't remember receiving.

The spades had possession of the ball when we resumed. I was angry—determined to exact revenge. That's when your judgment tunnels, of course, and you're most likely to compound mistakes. Fortunately, a play went by during which my muscles were able to siphon off most of the excess emotional steam. Again it was Morton, the flabby weirdo, who outdid himself. He'd learned a trick, and he repeated it. He looped a high pass to C.J., who, instead of burying the ball, flipped it back. The Cornell Kid was expecting that about as much as the rest of us. The ball caromed off his chest, almost bowling him over, but somehow he recovered it. With that skipping, effeminate motion of his, he shoved the ball up at the basket. It went in. Enough to turn your stomach. But it made the score 16–8.

I blotted my upper lip in the crook of my arm. Still dripping. The spade took the ball out. He passed to Pierre, who gave it back. I decided I had been playing him too tight. I hung off a few feet, hunched to respond in any direction. He dribbled—watching me, his stare feeling me up coldly from deep beneath his beetling ape brow. Black skin sweating greasily around the rheumy eyes. I glowered back.

Suddenly there was a flicker. I could sense the shift of tension to his thighs and calves. And then he was in the air, going up for his shot.

But so was I. Both arms flung high. Scrabbling for altitude as I drove to the limits of my reach with every foot-pound of bitter pride I could muster. My eyes were zeroed on the ball, muscles keyed to the sighting eyes. The ribbed sphere came off his fingers . . . and I smashed it! Baby, I smashed it hard and clean! Clawed it out of the sky and drilled it thirty feet down the court. I pirouetted lightly to the deck, avoiding contact as I landed. It was a perfect block. Flawless timing, no foul.

"Shiiiit," he drawled, "maaaan!" The pitch of his voice slid up-scale in disgust. He was looking down at himself, shaking his head. He didn't seem even to have noticed the block. He was intent, instead, on his shoe or something. No, now I saw what it was. A dime-size spatter of fresh blood glistened, bright and slimy, athwart the golden crease of his pants just above the knee. My blood, no doubt. Had to be. He drew back his lips and flared the broad wings of his nostrils even farther than normal. With dainty plucks of revulsion he peeled the offended fabric away from the skin beneath. His bony blue-edged teeth ground silent spade curses.

"Hm," I acknowledged. I offered a sheepish grimace and rolled my eyes. "Sorry about that."

"God*damn,* man!" he said. He squinted at me incredulously. Then he wagged his head some more.

I dragged the cuff of my sweatshirt over my wrist and leaned down to scrub at the stain.

He back-pedaled quickly away.

"I said," I shrugged, "I was sorry. I didn't do it on purpose."

Dick was watching us. He stepped nearer. "Maybe you *ought* to sit out for a little while, Dave. Until that bleeding stops."

The short spade shouldered closer. "Damn right. That's bad shit." His eyes were narrowed, and his cocoa features puckered pugnaciously. "Look at what you did there to the cat's pants."

"Yeah," I agreed, letting an answering belligerence creep into my own voice. "I can't help it if a guy wants to come out here and play in his good clothes. That's a risk of the game."

"Gonna cost him bread," C.J. rumbled.

"Christ," I replied, "any two-bit dry cleaner . . ."

"Really, Dave, you ought to take it easy." This was my solicitous, stinking guardian angel, Phil. "There's no sense in keeping on playing when you've got blood coming out like that."

" 'Blood coming out,' " I muttered. I wiped my nose and

lip on my shoulder. A narrow mucous stripe, crimson, glistened.

Morton dribbled into our midst with the ball he had gone to fetch. My great block was forgotten now . . . eclipsed by a triviality.

"Listen, friends"—I nodded—"I appreciate your deep concern. Only I'll decide when I'm too hurt to continue. . . ."

"Aw, that's hardly anything." It was Morton. He angled up close and appraised my nostrils. "Naah. It isn't even bleeding anymore. Come on, you're okay." He thumped me on the seat.

He was a beautiful little guy, the total asshole.

The spade produced a folded handkerchief from his hip pocket and mopped at my blood. You'd think, the way he flinched, he'd been defiled or something. He cast me an unhappy glance. I mugged another apology. The only thing else I could think of to do would be to offer to pay his cleaning bill. But I couldn't really bring myself to grips with the mechanics of that. So I stood apart, sulky, sleeking my ruffled temper on heroic mental replays of my championship defense. Fingering the rims of my nostrils to make sure they had actually quit leaking.

The light was growing considerably dimmer now. It wouldn't be long before we'd have to rely more on instinct than aim to guide our shots. Especially in this crepuscular pit. I had been sweating heavily under my clothes. I felt a sudden chill—shivered as bare bold air began to creep around the contours and into the crevices of my damp body. Hard to tell if it was getting colder out or I was just cooling down. The breeze was noticeably stronger. It had nowhere to go once it scuttled down the driveway. It just kicked around in swirls off the walls and corners. Dying dustily and badly.

"Come on, let's finish this off," I grumbled.

Morton backed behind the out-of-bounds line. There was a short, halfhearted disagreement about the score. We settled on 14–8, spades.

I was in aggressive fettle. I had gained, I told myself, a psychic advantage on my man. True, it had been necessary to scramble more visibly than I like to—to sweat more earnestness than I care to reveal into guarding him. And he had not yet, himself, it was true, lapsed from nonchalance. Still . . . Well, though, come to think of it, maybe he had. When he showed he was upset by my blood. In a way I was almost sorry I couldn't exploit that further: Okay, black boy, watch it . . . stand back or I'll sprinkle you with my contaminating white corpuscles. Like a mean kid with a dead mouse, exulting in his power over girls. Anyway, the thing to do next was to turn whatever advantage I might have into points. We were down six—and I had only shot once, even though I was undeniably the best gun on my team. I resolved to get the ball back and flip the game on end.

But the spades had a different idea. Morton inbounded to Pierre. Pierre passed off to my man. The spade danced outside, giving the play room to develop. I watched him warily. Ready to crowd him as soon as he edged into range. He swung left. I slid crosscourt with him. Suddenly he zigged back, picking up speed, driving toward the key. I sank into a deeper crouch and thrust a guarding hand before me. I whisked the other loosely behind my rump, feeling for blindside blockers.

"Pick right!" a warning voice called.

My rear hand smacked flesh. Immediately I crashed into a sweat-slick obstacle.

"Switch!" I cried.

The spade careened past, brushing me off neatly against Pierre, who had snuck up to screen. At my shout, Dick fell away with the spade. I had to cover Pierre now. I hooked him with an elbow and pivoted, throwing my hip into him for good measure, trying to knock him off-balance—or at least to hold him outside—until I could work my feet around between him and the basket. But he had the jump on me. He fought loose and broke for the pole. The spade's bounce-pass was perfection. There was nothing I could do except foul.

I gave him a shove between the shoulderblades—not even making a pretense at legality. He lost control of his momentum, regained it, managed to dodge the pole, but clattered heavily into the chain-link fence. He just succeeded in getting the ball up in front of him as a cushion.

"Sorry," I announced. "Take it. My foul."

Pierre's answering look was poisonous. He bent over and stared at the ground, bouncing the ball with sharp, vicious slaps. His thicket of tangled hair glinted greasily. When he looked up at me again he said, "You want to play basketball? Or . . . ?"

"Hey." I chuckled, conciliatory. "You had me. It was either that or two points. I didn't mean to put you through the fence, though."

"Yeah."

I turned my back on him. Set about guarding the spade on the inbounds play. T.S., you squat monkey, I thought. If you can't take a little standard roughing . . .

The spade began to bob. I hung close, maneuvering with

him, arms extended over my head to impair his view. I studied his eyes for the reflection of the ball's flight. Grunts and sibilances described the invisible movements unwinding behind me. The black irises I was watching floated sideways. I darted a peripheral glance that way, over my left shoulder. The spade's upper torso jerked right. I caught his motion in the other corner of my vision. My legs alertly launched me in response. But it was only a feint. He cut left, into the clear, and took the pass from Pierre. I recovered and surged back to pinch off his lane. Too late. He lowered his shoulder, hooked it like a bull in the soft cleft beneath my ribs, and sent me sprawling.

His shot erupted at the precise instant of impact. It crabbed off the board with a hoop-bound determination that was just this side of miraculous.

I squirmed on my chipped coccyx. Gasping for breath as my mouth filled with verbal acid. For a moment a black haze seemed to engulf me—belching up in acrid clouds from my sore chest, buzzing behind my eyes, swirling, even, outside me, as though wisps were escaping under pressure from my ears and throat and nostrils. It was a combination of shock, pain, oxygen starvation, and violent anger. And, enflaming it all the more . . . was the realization that in a game the foul would have been called on *me!*

I forced myself to my feet. The fog was clearing. I was not disabled to any serious degree—I had been traveling with the blow, and had broken my fall with the heels of my hands. Tiny raddled contusions—the warp of the asphalt—indented them. All right, I snarled to myself, if that's the way we're going to play, that's the way we're going to play! I dusted the seat of my pants and swallowed air hungrily.

"Come on, guys," Dick rallied us. He held up a metaphorically balled fist. "Let's get tough!"

Exactly.

Pierre inbounded the ball to Morton. Morton passed to the spade. I advanced, muscles knit. He fired it back to Pierre. Pierre fed C.J. C.J., well harried by Phil, missed his shot. Dick plucked off the rebound. He cleared the ball to Doug. At last we had it. . . .

"Hey! Here!" I shouted, prancing to stay open, semaphoring for attention.

Doug chose, instead, to dribble into trouble.

"Damn it all!" I bellowed. "Here! Pass!"

And so, finally, he reacted. He slung the ball at me sidearm. Full force, from about six feet. I ducked and threw up my hands—the reflex as much defensive as it was strategic. Even so, I barely managed to escape decapitation. The ball sizzled off my shoulder and continued, undeflected, on its hurtling course out of bounds.

I stood gaping. I blinked at Doug in a parody of owl-eyed astonishment.

He rattled the pea in his bullet skull dejectedly. "Aw, my fault," he lamented. "My fault."

I hung my head, looked away. Had to. I bowed and supported the burden of my sorrows with hands on knees. It was ridiculous, but it wasn't funny. Had I said this game was classy? Here we were, down eight points, and we had succeeded in controlling the ball for all of about eight seconds. What really galled, though, was the fact that technically I was responsible for the turnover. The ball had touched me last. Maybe I *should* have been able to handle it. But how was I to know the unconscious bastard was going to try to mow me down with it? . . . Aagh, shit! Exculpation and self-accusal tumbled like deadlocked wrestlers in my throbbing head. The problem was, I was wearing down. I hadn't played this hard in years. And all for a meaningless public-court game with anonymous antagonists. I sighed, rocked on my heels, and blubbed air resignedly through lax lips.

Pierre, a smug hint of derision tipping the straggly ends of his mustache, took the ball out. I covered the spade like clothes. Doug worried Morton. Finally C.J. advanced beyond the foul line. Pierre tossed to him. Phil moved up and held on cautiously. C.J. thought things over. Like a lot of very good tall players, he seemed vaguely embarrassed by his eminence. By the advantage his soaring height gave him over ordinary mortals—compounded by his very command of it. Against Phil, of course, he was matched in inches. But I didn't doubt that he could outmaneuver, outjump and outshoot Phil anytime he really chose. Sometimes that reluctance to exercise superiority is itself a disadvantage. And, too, sometimes what comes across as confident self-effacement is actually an artful cloak for mediocrity. Well, anyway, in C.J.'s case it was definitely not the latter. He swung the ball as if he meant to drive. Phil backed away at the ready, and instead, C.J. pumped. A tree with an outside eye. Phew. Deadly. His shot traveled downhill all the way.

So I had just about abandoned myself to defeat when Dick stole a pass. Pierre, supremely arrogant now, tried to feed C.J. at full throttle behind his back. Dick, trailing slightly, flagged the ball down and laid it up himself, unchallenged. It was a lucky break for us. Eighteen to ten. Maybe we could still come back.

Dick clapped his hands and chortled at his own prowess.

He galloped to the rear and called for the ball. I moved toward him, imploring mutely. Come on, man, here, to me. But my shamefully unsubliminal telepathy was being staticked under some kind of terrific jamming. The wall-eyed shit put the ball in play to Doug. I am not a glutton for humiliation. I subsided into a distant low-profile watchfulness. Doug had the intelligence, at any rate, to unload on Phil. Softly. And Phil clambered up over C.J. for a muscular goal.

I took the ball out. At least that way I could confirm what it felt like before the game ended. I lobbed it to Dick and shuffled disconsolately after the action. I did not expect to be a part of it. Wonder of wonders, though, Dick fired back. His pass had crackle. The slap of the pebbled surface against my palms was electric. Instantaneously my pique fizzled. Adrenal sparks quivered through my calves and biceps. I pivoted, hunched, and faced the spade. My elbows were compassed, ball sheltered deep on the curve of my waist. Okay, shine, I grimaced, now it's my turn to shine.

I swung my humped shoulders like a bison about to charge. Pawed the asphalt, sneered. Guess which way I'm going, star? I threw him a head fake, danced a double false step, rocketed right off my anchored foot. I had the advantage, all right, but I couldn't quite squeak by.

So okay, jig, you're as lithe in reverse as in high. Try this. I stopped dead. He braked, but not before I had won the space I was seeking. I jumped and shot.

Shit! It was centimeters light. The ball clanged the lip of the hoop. Everyone else had sagged under. Phil and C.J. climbed each other, flailing for the rebound. But it came off high and curled, like a yoyo, right back into my waiting hands.

I had the leisure for concentration. Ten-footer, one out of two, same spot, should be a cinch. I gave it plenty of backspin and a touch more arch.

Son-of-a-bitch, though! This time my shot yawed left!

C.J. easily vacuumed the rebound.

Goddamnit all! God . . . damn! Nothing was going right!

I scrambled over to guard the spade. He had the outlet from C.J. He brought the ball crosscourt, around the top of the key. Pierre set a pick. Dick and I switched off. Pierre dipped and darted—his game founded on the unflagging, infuriating endurance those midgets always seem to revel in. I despise gutsy little five-nine backcourt wizards. But I was just reckless and angry enough to hazard my evaporating reserves in an effort to smother him. At least my longer legs gave me a step's margin. I wheezed exhaustedly through sandpaper-lined orifices, and slapped and grabbed him for balance as often as I could. He reeked of sweat—a raw animal pungency I couldn't avoid as I sucked it deep into my chapped lungs. That smell I always associate with sparerib grease and squalid rooms and unwashed colored clothes. My hands slithered on his viscid skin. He whirled, trying to gyrate free. I saw, by the sudden fix of his eyes, a pass coming. I lunged and flung a hand in front of his groping hands. The ball struck my little finger. It jammed the knuckle painfully. But the spade, reading his own mistake, had followed like a mamba. He swept in the blocked ball and brushed past me before I could recoil. I twisted to chase—and stumbled over Pierre. His obstructionism was no mere accident. I lurched off my feet and fell . . . but not until I had clutched an avenging handful of shirt and jackknifed a knee hard into his ribs. I hung on and dragged him down beneath me as I toppled.

We rolled together on the ground. "Get . . . the fuck . . . off," he hissed, "me, you cocks . . ." He flung an elbow, half-punch, half-wriggle. I absorbed it with a shoulder. I forced him down, under my whole weight, trying to crush, to grate him against the sharp grain of the asphalt. He writhed. Too slimy to hold—it was like wrestling a slug. I pumped another knee into his kidney, and mashed my forearm into his windpipe as I levered myself half up, scrabbling for footing. A restraining arm suddenly snaked around me from behind.

"Come on! Cut the shit! Break it up, you guys!"

I was hauled erect, struggling. Phil had me. "Break it up, assholes!" he snapped. C.J. and Doug jumped between us. The swarthy little bastard milled arms and legs like a capsized roach. He aimed a toe at my vulnerable groin as I was hoisted away from him. I managed to intercept it on a ham.

"You dirty . . . !" The plosive snout of a racial adjective slammed into the breach of my cocked lips. But I spiked it off at the last millisecond. Thought better of that, here.

"Fucking dwarf," I muttered. More to myself than him. I had regulated my rage down to sullen. "If you were two feet taller I'd scrunch you into the size you are now, pissant!" I tried to shrug off Phil.

". . . Motherfuck can't play," Pierre's slow, snide whine drifted to me, "for shit." He had strutted away in the crescent of C.J.'s arm. They leaned together now, casual, conspiratorial. Mutt and Jeff in blackface.

"Christ," I demanded of Phil, "submarine a guy like that, what the hell does he expect?" I piped it loud and earnest. Then I knitted my fist and lowered my voice. "Bastard wants to fight, I'll fight!" But I did not want to fight. I was outraged innocence. "Shit," I said, "all I did was trip over him!"

"Come on, Dave, cool it," he soothed.

"Yeah, yeah." I stooped to catch my breath. I looked at my knuckle. Left hand, anyway. It was already puffy and discolored. I could still bend the finger, though.

"They score, I suppose?" I asked.

"Yeah." I felt the pressure of Phil's hand ease. Trail up the curve of my spine and disappear. He was satisfied, I guess, that I had cooled it. "Fed the little guy."

"Uh. Little guy?"

"Him." Phil nodded at Morton.

"Jesus," I spat, "Christ!" I swallowed the last syllable with a moan. Hung my head. I almost sobbed in frustration. I hadn't meant to assert my disdain so clearly. But this . . . just . . . somehow . . . this was just the last straw. The last fucking *straw!* Morton. Ho . . . Morton, shit! *shit!* That uncoordinated cluck, that limp Jew sack of laundry. Scored! Scored twice in this game now. Twice! And Doug. And everybody. Everybody but me, the superstar. I didn't even *look* good! I mean, Morton, the mobile jelly roll, he could put up a shot with the grace of a myocardial infarction, and the fucking goddamn thing would fucking *whisk* through the hoop. And this . . . this other walking disaster, this muscle-brained dimwit Doug . . . he was about .750 from the floor too. Holy hell! Holy *hell!*

I lashed at a white line with my rubber-shod toe. The line did not bend. I clenched my molars and screwed my eyes shut and sniffed searing drafts of air through my quavering nostrils. I could feel the dirt caking thick on the filtering cilia. Fucking grit, fucking shit . . . fucking everywhere. Fucking toxic air, fucking city, fucking black fucking bastards. Fucking everything!

Okay. Enough's enough, I gulped. Sighed. Come on, supernova, calm your palpitating organs. It's only a game, as we say. Not even a game. What does it matter? Will the Red Chinese care in a thousand years? No, chances are they will not. Nobody will care. Nobody will care that I ache from stem to sternum. That I am a bloody mess. That I have a purple knuckle and a bent nose and an overall coating of carcinogenic urban grime. And that I can't buy a basket. I'm just having an off-day. Everybody experiences that once in a while. Even the spade must. Sure, that's it, laugh at your foibles. Yuck it off. I know I'm good, basically. That's all that counts. I *am* good. In fact, it isn't even an off-day, really. I was hitting fine before. The spade knows it. He knows I'm good. There's a wind now. And even in this game I've stolen the ball from him. Well, knocked it away. And blocked a shot. And I'm certainly holding him down on points. Although he's holding me to zero. But that's because I'm shooting so fucking lousy. And anyway, I've only taken three shots. A dry spell, that's all. Can't score if you don't get the ball. Sometimes there just seems to be a lid on . . .

Et cetera.

Morton the Magnificent played the ball in. Twenty to twelve the score. As far as I was concerned, the game was over. Conceded. Anger is a function of caring, and if I wanted to douse my anger, the answer was not to care. No reason to, anyway. I couldn't save us single-handedly—and I was definitely not getting the cooperation I needed. Let the spades have their kicks. Drub the honkies. It's no lily-white skin off my aquiline nose. I could play right along with any one of those pongids if the teams were even. Certainly shoot rings around that goddamn quadroon runt Pierre. His cocksurety—

so fucking misguided—was what made me simmer! Like the spade, who knew his own ability and mine, I didn't care if he occasionally got the better of me. Have to expect that. But when some sawed-off splay-footed semiepileptic illiterate probably illegitimate unwashed fucking son-of-a-welfare-reject confuses blind luck and niggerly tricks with his own skill and a right to . . . denigrate . . . ah hell!

I glided along with the spade, perfunctory. He had the ball.

Give them their four points. Get it over with. If you don't try, I philosophized, you can't get your self-respect bootheeled.

I practically begged him, by my diffidence, to shoot. So he did. I flapped a weary finger at him in the way of defensive effort.

But, oddly enough, the ball ringed the hoop and popped clear. We sprang together for the rebound—pure reflex powering me. Forearms, hips, ankles clacking, we vied for a handle on the ball.

I managed to outstrain him. I came down with it . . . and immediately had the ball slashed out of my grip by Pierre. He had tiptoed around me from behind. He zipped to the foul line, fired to Morton, who fired to C.J., who flicked it to my man, who shoveled it to Pierre, who drove for a twisting layup.

The spades cackled. They bunched at midcourt, jiving. Slapping one another's palms. Even Morton got his mitt greased. "Way to work it in there, tiger." Pierre winked.

I stared blackly. He had fouled me. Swiped at least one-third flesh swiping two-thirds ball. But I wasn't going to give him the satisfaction of a whimper. I squinted at the strawberry bruise on the back of my right wrist. Discernible, actually, more by its dull sting than its discoloration. The darkness was closing in now. The murk thick enough to be cut by light. One of the windows high above us glowed faintly, and the diamond fence links on the right side of the court glittered with dim reflections of the streetlamp at the end of the driveway.

The spade took the ball out. Passed it to Pierre. Dick sparred with him as he dribbled.

There was nothing to lose. I abandoned my man and sprinted toward Pierre from the rear.

"Behind you!"

"Watch it!" C.J. yelled.

I intercepted the dribble just as Pierre jerked around evasively. It was absolutely clean—vengeance unsullied. The cow-flash of his startled eyes, the whinnying flare of his nostrils, should have been enough to warm me through winter. But I had something more vicious in mind. Instead of speeding away along the natural, direct route to the basket, I hesitated. Stepped back and flaunted my acquisition—hung it there in front of him . . . that one extra, tantalizing, lingering bounce of the ball.

And precisely as I had calculated, he hurled himself at it.

I sprang from my crouch. I caught him with the end of my collarbone flush on the point of the jaw. His flat face snapped back with a teeth-jarred click. Beadlets of thick nigger sweat spattered on my own grim face. A sharp bone-pang splintered, radiated along the marrow of my left shoulder.

But I was moving through the impact. I drove at the basket, wincing, rabid . . .

The spade cut across in front of me. His night-fighter

pigment almost blending him into the dusk. His gold undercarriage, churning, luminesced. A perfect target. I gritted my jaw and launched myself dead at him. Karate style—twisting in flight, knees drawn up to protect my crotch, leading foot locked in front, cocked left elbow flexed before my hip. I aimed at the top of his trousers. Heel-spurs to puncture the abdominal wall . . . puree his nuts . . . hipbone to shatter the laryngeal cartilage . . . elbow to smash the system, jelly an eye . . .

But he spun and ducked desperately. He hunched beneath me. I plunged into his bent back, ricocheted across. My shins snagged. Lagged. With sudden terror, I canted forward, pitching out of control. I had been cradling the ball at the ready in the shadow of my hip. Even now, as I corkscrewed into the vortex of my dive, some instinct triggered a shot.

My arm was almost wrenched out of its socket as the spade's blocking hand clamped down over the ball.

I plowed into the asphalt. I was able to wrap my skull and tuck into a comma before I hit. I absorbed the concussion across the yoke of my back. A searing reverse shock-image, like a negative—a fleeting worm's-eye perspective of gray skypatch, white buildings, black backboard and distorted minstrel faces—lurched across my vision. I cartwheeled to a stop, jangling, against the fence.

The basketball skittered after. Bounced loose, mockingly, beside me. Tap . . . tap . . . tap . . . tap . . . tap . . . Lazy, persistent, insinuating as a pickaninny's snigger.

I began to creep on hands and knees. Fumbled for the ball, hugged it to me. Abject, nearly insensate, conscious at first only of a bleak, barren, bottomless, apparently total and irredeemable frustration. As though my physical fall were being replayed, mirrored, interiorly. I was trapped in a sort of vertiginous vertical Laugh-in-the-Dark. Hurtling at terrifying speed through the mental blackness, past tiny illuminated tableaux: a bristling Mighty Joe Young claw clutching . . . a humiliating caricature of that last incredible block . . . amplified maniacal glee . . . a flock of grackles preening, flapping their wings . . . ebony beaks tearing at some limp pink carrion remnant . . .

And then my body joined in. Every tortured ligament, muscle, sinew, and bone murmured its complaint. The physical cacophony swelling. Becoming a hysterical bray for revenge. The harpy chorus mounting to a crescendo on the ominous inner hush . . .

And then the rage erupted. Boiling, hissing, screeching cyclonic fury. . . .

I leaped to my feet and heaved it at him. Blasted the ball with all my force at the spade's glistening face. I wanted only to obliterate him. Dissolve those impassive pig eyes, and polyp nose, those puckered purple lips on one orgasmic jet of primordial hate energy. See him explode with an apocalyptic gush of petroleous nigger blood and black bile and teeth and mucous and sweat and saliva and shredded gristle. . . .

But he was too fast. Or perhaps my vacillant mind finally and irrevocably betrayed me. Committed my body to murder, and then, at the ultimate instant, tried to snatch back the sanction. Maybe the milk-blood stagnating in my cerebral veins had grown too dilute over the soft centuries. All chalky sediment now—lymph and lies.

I flinched.

Morton couldn't have seen it coming. He was screened behind the spade until the spade dodged. The ball smashed into his fragile moonface just as he turned. Beard-framed bull's-eye. An awful, stricken, mushy clap resonated. Followed instantaneously by a throaty gong. The chord hung in the air . . . its every fractured dissonance pealing in the pit of my gut as Morton, his face a scarlet syrup and his skullshell cracked through by the iron pole, slid to the ground.

I heard the click then. Saw the glint of *steel*. I don't know which one of them it was, though.

And then I screamed as the obscene blade probed, butter-soft, into my bowels. . . .

Thomas A. Boswell

The Shooter

The sports Americans have created, and still love best, all hinge on the flick of a wrist.

The spiral of a forward pass, the biting snap of a curveball, the soft backspin of a jump shot are the hallmarks of our indigenous team games.

Among our native creations—football, baseball and basketball—perhaps there is no central weapon as democratic, yet undeniably aristocratic, as the jump shot.

Everybody's got one, but they sure aren't equal. Occasionally a shooter can be made. But mostly they're born. The gift of "touch" is a silver spoon, even if it is discovered on the bleakest playgrounds.

The shot—its quality and purity—is the gold standard of the hoop world. The gifted shooter carries with him a sense of princely authority, a kind of regal legerdemain. To any predicament, he has the solution. Possessor of an invisible scepter, he is an heir to adulation.

"When you feel a streak comin' on, you become unconscious; you feel like you could lie on your back, close your eyes, and it would go in," says George Washington University coach Bob Tallent, who has the highest scoring average (28.9) of any major college player in Washington area history (as a Colonial in 1968–69).

"You could feel ten or eleven in a row comin' on," says Tallent. "When you get like that, it doesn't matter what defense they're in, or who's on your team. The rest of the game fades away.

"You get hot and that's it. The game belongs to you until you cool down. You know what you're doing and where you are, but it's like you're in a trance, or surrounded by some kind of aura."

Most of basketball humanity has to blend and flow, fitting into a five-man jazz ensemble where the riffs are shared and the harmony, not the solos, is what matters.

But the shooter always senses a higher possibility, the chance to wire into the collective fantasies of the crowd.

"Every fan is just waiting to get on your wavelength and give you their energy," says Tallent.

"The shot is a total motion, a groove. No two shooters are alike, but they feel the same when they're on," says Kevin Grevey of the Washington Bullets, lifelong bomber and NBA "H-O-R-S-E" semifinalist.

"With a crazy streak shooter like me, one or two baskets will trigger me. I'll start throwing them in from everywhere. It pumps up your whole game. You do everything better and your confidence and concentration are total." Like any gunslinger, the shooter has his nightmares.

"What you do to others, they can do to you," says

Grevey. "If Cazzie Russell missed his first few shots, he'd play terrible defense all night. If he made his first one, he was like a man possessed.

"The in-your-face guys can drive you crazy. When Doug Collins [of Philadelphia] got hot against me in the playoffs one year [28 points in one half], I felt like that cartoon character Ricochet Rabbit. I thought I was a ball caught inside a pinball machine.

"When they shoot you down, you just want to hide."

The quarterback and the pitcher—those other protagonists in our most common athletic fantasies—always have forces working in opposition to them. They are always at the mercy of others to some degree, whether teammates or foes.

The shooter is the most nearly solitary of our team heroes. At his instant of truth, after he has dribbled, driven or scraped off a screen, there is nothing in his universe except the ball in his hand, the rim in his eye and the righteousness born of a lifetime's practice in his heart.

"Shooters are oblivious," says Catholic University coach Jack Kvancz. Sometimes it seems like they don't think at all. They don't get the sweaty palm.

"When the game gets tight, they want it. They want it when everybody else is glad to give it up. Shooters, as a group, aren't even the best athletes on the team.

"How do you make people like that?"

Tallent knows where the making of a shooter starts. When he was twelve years old, growing up in the mountains of eastern Kentucky, where every Appalachian peak seemed to produce a Zeke from Cabin Creek, Tallent came under the sway of "King" Kelly Coleman.

"All shooters start by imitation," says Tallent. "I hitchhiked thirteen miles each way so I could rebound for him and throw the ball back to him. I was in the sixth grade and he was averaging 18 points a game for Waylon High.

"Like all shooters, there were lots of tall tales about King Kelly, some of 'em pretty-near true.

"Adolph Rupp said he was better than Frank Ramsey and Cliff Hagan combined. So that's all you need to know," says Tallent. "But Kelly had a wild streak. Oblivious on the court and off it.

"I remember them throwing him in the shower for the whole first half of a high school game. He scored 42 in the second half.

"When he played my school, we double-teamed him from the moment he stepped off the bus. We held him to 75 points," said Tallent.

"He was a big sloppy-looking guy—6 foot 4, 220 pounds," recalls Tallent.

"But he could do anything. One time they booed him for three nights in a row in the state tournament, even though he scored 52, 46, and 29.

"He was crying after the third game and told the reporters, 'By God, I'll show these city people. I'll score 70.'

"He didn't, though," says Tallent. "He only got 68. But it's still the state tournament record."

Every area of America, from Iowa to Far Rockaway to Turkey Thicket playground in Northeast Washington, has its King Kellys. For every long-distance runner, there are hundreds who savor the loneliness of the long-distance shooter, practicing from the moment the sun rises over the mountain or the tenement.

"The only generalization you can make about shooters is

that they can all put in the hole," says Bobby Dandridge of the Bullets. "There are pure shooters, improvisational shooters like me, mechanical shooters like Elvin Hayes and guys like George Gervin with weird releases.

"I never went to any basketball camps," says Dandridge with an appropriate curl of the lip. "I don't know any of that jive about fingertips and watching the rim and making your arm look like a box.

"I'm a playground scorer. I don't have a shot. I have many shots," says the owner of 15,000 NBA points.

"I may change my release two or three times a season. Sometimes I don't know if I release the ball with one hand or two. I go on my emotions. If my emotions say I'm going to make the shot, then I'm going to make it."

The inside of a shooter's mind is the last frontier. Perhaps no aspect of any sport is as inexplicably streaky as shooting. Whole teams go hot and cold, defying probability by being both incredibly good and bad in the same game.

"Practice is different from games, and even various parts of the game are different," says Kvancz. "Some guys can shoot at four P.M., but not eight. And some can shoot at eight, but not in the final minutes.

"I don't coach perfect form because, in the clutch, the elbow sticks out, the feet kick and the kid reverts to all the habits he's had all his life. I tell 'em, 'Drop-kick it in if you have to. Shoot the way it's comfortable, not the way that looks good, because it's mostly in your mind anyway.' "

In fact, the basket is rather wide. It is the mind that is narrow. If the hoop were only four inches wider, two balls could go through it at once.

"It's scary to see a good shooter go bad," says Kvancz.

"One year, Glenn Kolonics [a top scorer at CU] was going so rotten that I ordered him to grow a beard. I told him he couldn't shave until he had a good shooting game.

"Well, Kolonics looked like Grizzly Adams before he ever got his touch back."

"I remember the shot when he got it back," says Tallent. "Kolonics came into our gym in January with this full beard. His first shot hit the back rim, bounced about ten feet straight up and swished on the way down.

"That was it. You could see his eyes wake up. He lit us up for about 32 that night."

Most great shooters know they will be roughed up, punched, gouged and elbowed. It comes with the turf. And most react as Jerry West once did.

"Kentucky put in a big old horse named Allen Feldhaus to do some enforcing against West when he was at West Virginia," says Tallent. "In two minutes, Feldhaus had broken West's nose and sent him to the dressing room.

"Jerry came back in the second half with a face mask on and scored 24 points. When you get the good ones angry, it just helps their concentration. When you're mad, sometimes you think you'll never miss again. Pat [Tallent] and I both kinda liked it rough."

Perhaps the most despised shooters are not the streakers or the guys who talk trash or even those who seem to shoot better the more closely they are guarded. The worst are the shooters who add injury to insult.

"I used to hate Zelmo Beaty," says Bullet Wes Unseld. "He couldn't jump much and he couldn't shoot too well if he was closely guarded. So he worked out a shot to keep defenders away from him.

"His release was designed so that his follow-through would clobber you in the face. He slugged me hundreds of times for free."

"The worst at that today is Lloyd Free," says Unseld's teammate Greg Ballard. "He's got his leg kick at the end of his shot perfected so that he kicks you in the groin. Then he's the one who falls down, rolls around and gets the foul called his way."

A whole language has grown up around the jumper: jack it up, stop-and-pop, shoot the J, fire the pill, shoot the rock, run-and-gun, hoist it, fill it up.

The permutations never end.

"They call me the Heist Man," says Barry Frazier, who was a 35-point-a-game jump shooter for the small-college University of the District of Columbia. "Why? Because I can really heist it."

Those occasional dark hours come when the shot disappears.

"Sometimes you think you couldn't throw it in the ocean," says Grevey. Adds Tallent, "I can't believe it but even Brian Magid [of GW] has gone into a slump. He's seven for his last thirty-one, and he's got the longest range I've ever seen."

But for the shooter the dawn always comes.

"You get alone in the gym and say, 'Think soft,' " says Grevey. "You see how many shots you can get off in thirty seconds. That way, you don't have time for flaws. You go back to your old instincts."

Or, like Bill Bradley, you start with lay-ups and never shoot from more than ten feet until you have made twenty-five in a row and thus reinforced your confidence.

Finally, the shooter gets the one break he needs—a sloppy roll, or a bounce that goes straight up, then down and through. Suddenly, the fantasy, the dream of a thousand solitary hours, becomes a temporary reality.

"You're hot," says Tallent, remembering. "You and the crowd have a special relationship. They call you a gunner, and they never give you credit for the other parts of the game that you can play. But when you're hot, they're all with you.

"Was I a gunner?" Tallent laughs, the chuckle of a shooter. "Hell, yes. You're cocky. You can't believe it if you miss. You feel unstoppable.

"I always knew that if I had room, if I could see the basket, it was goin' up. And the hell with what anybody thought."

Does that touch ever leave? Can Rabbit Angstrom, years later, running through the back alleys of John Updike's mind, always pick up the ball from schoolchildren and recapture the sweet loneliness of the long jumper?

Tallent smiles. "It never leaves."

Dick Wimmer

The Ultimatum of Hattie Tatum

Hattie Tatum stood 6′2 in sneakers. She'd been the center for the girls basketball team of her all-black high school in Spartanburg, South Carolina, had twice won all-State honors, and was generally considered an exceptional athlete. Following graduation, however, her mother had died, and, being poor, she and her older sister Cora decided to move north to find employment. Cora had a classmate working in Great Neck, so they headed there, registered with the Ring-a-Maid agency, and a week later, both had jobs: Cora in Harbor Hills and Hattie with the Levitases of Steven Lane. After a month, though, Cora, fed up, was fired and went home, leaving Hattie alone in Kings Point.

The house, a sprawling split-level ranch with Grecian columns, had recently been bought by Shelly with the windfall from his in-laws' estate, but was mortgaged up to the hilt—as his wife kept constantly reminding him. Yet to him it was a dream come true, finally living in the town's most exclusive section, and didn't Ro now have her best friend, Carole Friske, around the corner and, of course, Marcia Levy always at hand. Vance, their oldest child, was ten, and Lisa, seven and a half. Both were tall for their age, Vance extremely bright and taken with sports, and Lisa, a tomboy, detesting frillies or dress-up clothes. Just last week, Shelly had installed a basket at the far corner of his driveway and directly facing his garage, thus leaving thirty feet for playing space. The masonite basket was low, only eight feet high, had an orange rim, blue and white net, and cost him $9.95 at Korvettes. On a Saturday afternoon, he and Vance had crowded into Sporting Goods and Shelly'd picked the next-to-cheapest, a moderate choice, it looked good enough.

When Hattie arrived, the children hardly noticed. They'd had maids in the past; why should this one be any different? Only she was as big as their father and skinny as a pole. Hattie was friendly but reserved, and the children found they could do pretty much what they liked with her; she was no disciplinarian. But the housework was another matter. She never seemed able to please Mrs. Levitas, and it took two weeks before she could fully adjust to her "system." Rochelle, a management major while at Simmons, stressed that word, everything had to be done with a system, otherwise nothing was accomplished at all.

Under Rochelle's guidance, Hattie began to settle into the family routine. She had her own room, a small, narrow cubicle off the laundry room, an old RCA ten-inch TV, and a chest of drawers. It was removed from the rest of the house, so she had relative privacy, except when Shelly washed his softball uniform or the children raced past in games of tag. Hattie, though, was constantly at Rochelle's beck and call.

Any time was acceptable for her directions or orders of the day. "I'm going out now, Hattie, and I'll be back at three. If anyone calls, I'm at the hairdresser's. And if it's Mrs. Friske, tell her I'll see her at the game." Hattie often as not forgot these messages, and, under Rochelle's continued guidance, began yet another system, namely, jotting them down—Rochelle purchasing a pad and magnetic gold pencil for note-taking.

Meals, too, were a problem. She was constantly forgetting the A-1 sauce or ketchup for Mr. Levitas, and Lisa usually wanted cola instead of 7-Up or 7-Up instead of root beer. Hattie, of course, ate after, but it was lamb and pork chops like she'd never tasted and occasionally even leftover steak, always more than enough; and though she was never inclined to gain weight, she'd added six pounds after a month.

School would be over soon, the summer soon beginning, and when told she was to take the children outdoors during the afternoon and watch them, Hattie was delighted. They had a large backyard, but as the sun continued to shine, Vance decided he'd rather be playing basketball. So Hattie would stand behind him while he pushed or threw up his shots, hard flings that Hattie retrieved: the feel of the ball again, its smooth, grainy texture, so fine in her hands. But she never shot, just watched—while Lisa was given her one chance in five—or retrieved the ball for Vance.

After a week of this, as her ache to play kept growing, an opportunity finally arose. Vance had flung a wild hook down the drive, Hattie off in pursuit of the ball. But when she returned, the children had moved to the back lawn and were involved with their toy soldiers, leaving Hattie, ball in hand, alone on the court. She looked around. Mrs. Levitas was still at her husband's game, no cars passed, the children were sprawled now on the warm grass, and Hattie held the ball. She looked around again, walking down the drive to check if any maids were out or other children coming—no, not a soul. She couldn't stand it much longer. Every day the feel and bounce of the ball and never being able to shoot. It was overwhelming. Just last week on her day off, she'd gone into Corona to meet Cora's friend, who took her to a nearby Y. But it had been a tiring trip and she'd arrived home later than usual, when the children were asleep. So the chances seemed remote of doing that again. But now she held the ball in her palm and the court was clear. She bounced it twice—the children hadn't noticed—then cut toward the basket, dribbling behind her back and on out to the foul line, a faint chalk scrawl, stepped forward and tossed up her favorite shot, a long, looping one-hander that went swishing cleanly through, gathered in the ball and moved to the corner, along the rock border of the drive, for a sweeping right-hand hook. By this time, Vance had turned and, seeing Hattie gracefully glide over the asphalt, was transfixed. On and on she played, the children abandoning their toy soldiers and sitting against the garage door to watch Hattie spin down the center lane and bank the ball in—and whirling round, coming face-to-face with the two of them.

She was embarassed, offering the ball to Vance, who shook his head. "I didn't know you played, Hattie. Why didn't you tell us?"

"Here, come on, you shoot."

"No, we wanna watch *you*."

"Please, don't stop!"

So Hattie played on, pausing every once in a while to

show Vance how to hold the ball, to shoot a long, looping one-hander, to balance it on the palm, then arch it softly; and with Lisa, teaching her how to dribble, to watch the ball and not just slap at it. The afternoon was growing late, it was now nearly five, and as the mothers and deliverymen drove by, many paused at the sight of this tall black girl dribbling between two small children who giggled and grasped to snare the elusive ball that flickered past on its ultimate way through the hoop. Till Hattie saw them too, and stopped, telling the children they had to go in.

"*NO, NO!* Just one more shot, Hattie, just one more!"

"All right, just one more."

"Bet you can't dunk it," challenged Vance.

"Well lemme see, 'cause at this height, I guess I might," and down the center lane she drove, soared high into the air and slammed the ball through the cords, the children crying, shrieking with delight, and embracing Hattie as they moved indoors.

Rochelle knew nothing of what had occurred; it was their own special secret. But as the weeks passed and school drew to a close, basketball was to become their daily play, hurrying home for a game of Horse or more often watch as Hattie revealed her talent. For talent it was—it had never left her—and Hattie was overjoyed. She would race through her housework, doing it now in half the time. Her weight soon back to normal, she could feel the spring returning to her legs, the touch to her fingertips with each passing day. By now Vance had developed a pretty good one-hander and Lisa at least could dribble in a straight line, but it still was Hattie's show. And show she did, performing acrobatic leaps and jumps, spinning the ball off her index finger, and always finishing with her resounding dunk. So absorbed were they that none of them had noticed the neighbors' blinds bending back, the drapes opening a wee bit, and the cars slowly pausing; for Hattie was becoming known throughout the neighborhood and Great Neck at large. But Shelly and Rochelle knew nothing, only that their children were happier than they had ever seen them with any previous maid, far better behaved, ate all their food at dinnertime, cleaned up afterward—and so, except for Hattie forgetting as usual, had very few complaints.

The following Tuesday, though, Rochelle nearly caught them. Hattie was throwing up a long one-hander as she approached the drive. "Hattie, how come you were shooting and the children were just sitting around?" Vance had interrupted to say that she was just showing them how it should be done when the phone rang, and Rochelle forgot completely about it as Carole chattered on.

But a week later, under the hair dryer at André's, she overheard two women discussing this *schvartze* who played basketball in Kings Point. "A maid, too—gets away with murder. You should hear what they say. . . ."

And the following day, when Colandro, her dry-cleaning man, asked how "Goose" Tatum was doing, Rochelle asked who "Goose" Tatum was. "A basketball player, Mrs. Levitas, used to be with the Harlem Globetrotters, almost as good as your maid."

That Friday, she told Hattie she was going to the city with Carole and would be back no later than five. However, she returned at four, the sun of June still shining, and passed slowly by. O my God! There she was *again*. Shooting! And the kids just standing around! Neighbors' eyes were peering out through their blinds, the next-door maid, hand on hip, mop in hand, was brazenly watching, and across the street, Denise Wanderstock, whose husband was head of the School Board, was laughing in her flower bed, obviously delighting in the spectacle. Rochelle sped down Steven Lane, nearly knocking over someone's black footman statue with her U-turn, and roared back up her driveway, screeching to a halt not three feet from Hattie and the kids!

After the irate lecture, Hattie stopped for a week, but at the kids' insistence sneaked out the following Saturday and shot for two hours, with Vance, Lisa, and Colandro keeping watch.

But the reports kept flowing in. Some no doubt malicious, from other maids jealous of Hattie's situation, though she had never worked harder, even learning to serve now with a sense of quiet style. Rochelle warned her again, saying it was the children's court, and she couldn't let this continue. A maid's job was not to play basketball. "No other maid does it. You don't have to. There's no need."

Hattie tried to explain how much the children enjoyed it, how much she needed it, how it improved her work—"Yes, but it doesn't look good for the maid to be playing and the children just sitting around. It isn't right. And all the neighbors watching."

"Well, we just play for a few hours—"

"No, you just *watch* the children, that's your job, I don't wanna discuss it anymore!"

That night, as *The Late Late Show* came on above Shelly's snuffling snore, Rochelle, nervously puffing on a Tareyton, thought about her neighbors, her husband's mounting debts (if only they knew!), and his wheeling and dealing, from shoes to fabrics to the used carpet business, staying in Great Neck at all costs—and yet even she had to admit how happy she was here in their luxurious Kings Point home. How much had they paid—what, 168? Yes, but that was last winter. Now it was easily worth another 50–60 grand. Lou's father, Sollie Grossbard, just two houses down and without a finished basement, sold his three years back for 143.5—and that after only a month on the market, straight cash! And she has her own room with a TV yet and the run of the house besides! Who's ever home? *Miss* Tatum, the Grand *Dame*! Give them a little freedom and they think they own the world! What more do they want? She makes more than all her relatives put together down in South Carolina or wherever the hell she comes from! All of them now talking back, big mouth she has on her, telling me what she wants! Who does she think she is? Like we haven't treated her nice. What more could we do? Gave her a house, food, clothes, buy her gifts on her birthday—a cake for $6.50 from Benkert's—and how much work does it take to clean this house? I used to do it in two hours, and her it takes all afternoon! And it still isn't clean, always dust under everything, no system. And a few meals a week to prepare? We usually eat out twice a week anyway after the games. And the kids, both at school till three, go to sleep at nine. And what's more, Thursday she's off, one day a week, the same as the rest of them. Gets home at God knows when, sometimes even Friday morning, and we never say anything. Shelly never even *talks* to her, who *bothers* her? She can do what she likes, whatever she wants. She has this whole $200,000 house to herself and she wants to play basketball. Basketball! Who ever heard of such a thing? You never even *see* the other maids, they're all busy working—just my *shvartze*! I have to get one from Spartanburg, South Carolina, who thinks she's a performer. Telling you, the trouble with help today!

But Hattie persisted. What else did she have? Cora wouldn't be back now till late September. Maybe when she'd put enough money away, she could enroll at a community college, but for now her only pleasure, besides the children, was basketball, those odd hours when she could sneak in a few shots and, best of all, replay those high school games of her past.

Shelly couldn't care less. He wanted a maid, a clean house, dinner served on time and generally well prepared—he'd add his own spice—and more important, harmony at home, so Ro would stop nagging him and let him have some peace. But now even *he* had begun to hear little stories about his basketball-playing maid. She was becoming well known, a snide joke at Glen Oaks and among nearly everyone at the games. Who else had a maid jumping around, throwing in baskets? It was ridiculous. People gossiping, it didn't look good, soon that'd be all they'd talk about! But what really bothered him was that this was his *home* and this scrawny, gawky *shvoog* (he always liked that better than *nigger*, that was crass, but *shvoogeedoogie* had a certain flair) was running around outside in full view of the neighbors! Like (God forbid!) she was his kid! Who knows what they might think, his lovely neighbors, four-flushers all! Some distant relative, niece or what, his own illegitimate daughter? The kid from some Negro show doll he'd been shtooping, like Leslie Uggams? He and Bucky'd put money in that *facoctah shvoog* review, *Hallelujah, Baby,* lost his shirt! Who knew what they were thinking? This on top of the rest of his worries, debts mounting, Ro and her nagging, his prostate acting up, hemorrhoids, too!

So, Sunday night before *Bonanza* (Shelly's favorite show) came on, Hattie was summarily told. She was called into the den, Rochelle asked to leave, no interruptions, and he snapped off the set.

"How-why-ya, Hattie—listen, there's been a lot of stories—it doesn't look good—the kids just sit around—and I know you get along well with Vance—but the neighbors—I mean the basket is his." Concluding, he lit up a Tiparillo, smoothing down his ringleted hair, and gave her Monday off, he'd make his own breakfast—and settle the housework chores with his wife.

Hattie was cowed. She said she'd try.

And for two weeks she did try. But after a daily diet of quiz shows and cooking shows, soap operas and vintage movies, cards, crosswords, and solitaire, of sheer boredom and repeated cleanings, she asked Mrs. Levitas again. Rochelle's reaction was silence. She had thought the matter closed. She called Shelly's office. He couldn't be bothered now, the rug merchants were driving him crazy, he'd call her back. But she had to wait two hours, and during that time she called Carole, Marcia (who, as usual, wasn't home), and the local agency, found a girl was available on Monday—this was Friday—and told Hattie, upon the advice of friends and family, she was letting her go.

Hattie, though aware of the possibility, still was shocked. She had grown to like Great Neck, the quiet, clean, tree-shaded streets, and especially the kids. But she couldn't just sit around like the rest of the maids and housewives. If she worked here, she had to have use of the basket.

So Hattie left. Vance wasn't home at the time. But when he returned and Hattie was nowhere in sight, he asked his mother if Thursday wasn't her day off. Was Hattie sick? "No, dear, she's no longer with us."

"Why?"

"Because—well, because there are certain things we just didn't see eye-to-eye on. I know you liked her very much, but don't worry, there'll be another girl here Monday and things will be just the same as—"

"I want *Hattie*!"

"Look, dear, I know—"

"*No!* Nobody else!"

"Vance, listen—"

"It's not *fair*!" And Vance stormed off into his room and slammed the door. Rochelle started after him when the phone rang. It was Shelly to say he'd be home late tonight, had a meeting with Justin Friske, a possible deal cooking. She told him what had happened, Vance's reaction, and he told her to forget about it. "Hattie, Schmattie, we'll have a thousand maids, tomorrow he won't even remember who she was!"

But the next day Vance shot baskets by himself. Long, looping one-handers indifferently thrown toward the hoop, head down, his eyes rimmed with tears. That night at dinner, he wouldn't eat, and when Lisa started kidding him, calling him a crybaby, he fired a baked potato at her—and was told to go to his room. He wouldn't talk to the new maid, an older woman with a ducal bosom who rolled her r's as in New Yo*r*k and was all for segregation. By this time, Lisa had joined

Vance in refusing to talk to the new maid, who told Rochelle she'd run up against this before with children and to just let them brood it out, ignore them, and they'd eventually come around. But three days passed, as Vance and Lisa remained disconsolate, barely touching their food, and Rochelle was now at her wits' end.

"Shelly, we can't live like this. Vance has lost five pounds already, he doesn't talk to me, or to the new maid, just stays in his room, won't even *play* basketball anymore, and Lisa is the same way! What're we going to *do*?"

Shelly, who still had carpets and debts but most of all softball on his mind and couldn't stand any more domestic upheavals, said he'd talk to the kids tomorrow.

But when tomorrow came, Vance and Lisa were gone. They'd slipped out during the early morning hours and by noon had reached the train station, where Dennis Hickey, on duty in his cab, turned them over to a cop, who drove them home. Shelly and Rochelle were beside themselves. They had awakened to a childless house and a carefully scrawled note: IF HATTIE GOES, WE GO TOO.

Shelly thanked the officer, offering him a tip, which was refused, then took his children into the den. "Look, this's gotta stop right now. Hattie is only a *maid*, you have your own lives to live. I know how much you liked her, but you still have each other, your mother and me." Vance and Lisa just stared down at the floor. "I don't even know where Hattie is now, she could be anywhere, probably back in South Carolina for all I know—Vance, are you *listening* to me?" Vance glanced up, then his eyes shifted away, as Shelly continued to boil. "From now on, you will eat when we eat and play with your own friends. I'm not gonna be aggravated by your foolishness, young man, is that clear? All right, go kiss your mother."

But though the children made halfhearted attempts to seem happy, their feelings remained unchanged. Vance had lost nine pounds, Lisa'd caught a cold, and the new maid was becoming lackadaisical in her cleaning and was constantly overcooking the meals. Finally, Rochelle couldn't take it anymore. Because of this *schvartze* and her basketball, her home was falling apart. Shelly was more irritable, she was now smoking nearly three packs a day, the house was a mess, and the kids were as thin as toothpicks. Something had to be done! She called the agency, but they wouldn't have another maid till the middle of next week. Carole Friske offered to lend her hers, though only for a few days, any longer was out of the question. "These kids and their maids. Mine was the same way, but they usually get over it—this I never heard of!"

There was only one thing to do: get Hattie back at all costs. She told Shelly. "Now you *want* her back? What the hell's with you? This day, this, next day, that. Ro, make up your mind already!"

"My mind is made up, Hattie has to come back, otherwise we'll both be nervous wrecks!"

"And what about the basketball?"

"We'll discuss it."

Rochelle still had that number in Corona, some friend of Cora's where she could be reached, but Hattie was out, down at the schoolyard. "Then please, have her call this number immediately! It's Mrs. Levitas—Levitas with an L—from Great Neck!"

"Yes, ma'am."

A half hour later, Hattie, still out of breath, called. "Hattie, listen, can you come back?"

"Come *back*?"

"Yes, we've changed our minds, can even give you a raise."

"How are Vance and Lisa?"

"Fine, fine. Listen, do you want to come back or not?"

"Well, I don't know—"

"You don't know, whatta you mean you don't know?"

"Well I may've another job."

"Another job? Where? What kinda other job? Here, in Great Neck, what part?"

"The junior high school . . ."

"*Junior high school? Our* junior high school? Doing what?" (Janitor? Custodian? Dishwasher?)

"Girls basketball coach."

"*Coach*? But how'd you get—?"

"Mrs. Wanderstock got me an interview, this afternoon at three."

"But don't you need a degree, credentials?"

"No, guess nobody else applied, so they decided to—"

"OK, OK, but you'll still need a place to stay, so take the next train out, I'll pay for it, pick you up, and we'll discuss all the details when you arrive."

Rochelle picked her up, discussing the details along the way. "But couldn't you still be a *part-time* maid?"

"And play basketball outside with the children?"

"Well . . ." and they swung into the drive just as Vance and Lisa came home, saw Hattie, and went shrieking into her arms.

It was decided, terms were agreed upon, with Hattie

rehired immediately part-time at twice her former wage. The sun kept shining as Vance and Hattie passed the ball back and forth while Lisa watched. Lisa went dribbling through Hattie's legs while Vance watched. Then it was Hattie's turn. The curtains of the neighbors edged back; she was about to perform. Holding the ball in one hand, Hattie spun it up to her index finger and let it whirl. Vance cheered, the ball spun on, Lisa giggled with glee. And then Hattie dribbled back of the key, drove hard to her right and tossed up her long, looping one-hander—Swish!

Cries of joy. On she played as more blinds were bent and cars paused, a dazzling array of shot-making: hooks, behind-the-back lay-ups, banked-in jumpers, two-hand bombs from thirty feet, and, at this low height, a final, soaring, rim-rattling dunk, *whomp*, through the blue and white cords!

Philip Roth

From Goodbye, Columbus

"... and by the time the first snow had covered the turf, it was the sound of dribbling and the cry *Up and In!* that echoed through the fieldhouse ..."

Ron closed his eyes.

"The Minnesota game," a new, high voice announced, "and for some of our seniors, their last game for the red and white ... The players are ready to come out on the floor and into the spotlight. There'll be a big hand of appreciation from this capacity crowd for some of the boys who won't be back next year. Here comes Larry Gardner, big Number 7, out onto the floor, Big Larry from Akron, Ohio ..."

"Larry—" announced the P.A. system; "Larry," the crowd roared back.

"And here comes Ron Patimkin dribbling out. Ron, Number 11, from Short Hills, New Jersey. Big Ron's last game, and it'll be some time before Buckeye fans forget him ..."

Big Ron tightened on his bed as the loudspeaker called his name; his ovation must have set the nets to trembling. Then the rest of the players were announced, and then basketball season was over, and it was Religious Emphasis Week, the Senior Prom (Billy May blaring at the gymnasium roof), Fraternity Skit Night, E. E. Cummings reading to students (verse, silence, applause); and then, finally, commencement:

"The campus is hushed this day of days. For several thousand young men and women it is a joyous yet a solemn occasion. And for their parents a day of laughter and a day of tears. It is a bright green day, it is June the seventh of the year one thousand nine hundred and fifty-seven and for these young Americans the most stirring day of their lives. For many this will be their last glimpse of the campus, of Columbus, for many many years. Life calls us, and anxiously if not nervously we walk out into the world and away from the pleasures of these ivied walls. But not from its memories. They will be the concomitant, if not the fundament, of our lives. We shall choose husbands and wives, we shall choose jobs and homes, we shall sire children and grandchildren, but we will not forget you, Ohio State. In the years ahead we will carry with us always memories of thee, Ohio State . . ."

Slowly, softly, the OSU band begins the Alma Mater, and then the bells chime that last hour. Soft, very soft, for it is spring.

There was goose flesh on Ron's veiny arms as the Voice continued. "We offer ourselves to you then, world, and come at you in search of Life. And to you, Ohio State, to you Columbus, we say thank you, thank you and goodbye. We will miss you, in the fall, in the winter, in the spring, but some day we shall return. Till then, goodbye, Ohio State, goodbye, red and white, goodbye, Columbus . . . goodbye, Columbus . . . goodbye . . ."

John Feinstein

From A Season on the Brink: A Year with Bobby Knight and the Indiana Hoosiers

Two weeks after the Cleveland State loss, Knight had not stopped brooding. He had made life miserable for the players during the first two days of their postseason practices, sitting in the stands while they scrimmaged. He even yelled at Bartow and Dakich for doing a poor job of refereeing on that first Sunday. When he left for Dallas on Thursday to go to the Final Four, everyone breathed a sigh of relief. The assistants ran scrimmages until the following Monday—the last day allowable under NCAA rules.

In Dallas, Knight was reunited with his coaching family. This is an annual affair, because the Final Four is also the site of the National Association of Basketball Coaches convention.

Knight rooms each year with Pete Newell, and he spent the weekend with people like Fred Taylor, Henry Iba, Bob Murray, and all his former assistants. On Friday night, the annual family dinner was held at a local Italian restaurant.

Knight spent a good deal of time during that weekend with Mike Krzyzewski, whose Duke team reached the championship game before losing to Louisville, 72–69. Knight wore a Duke button everywhere he went, spoke to Krzyzewski's team about playing in the Final Four, and went to Krzyzewski's room after the final to console him. There was irony here: Knight would have been inconsolable after such a loss, yet he insisted on trying to help console Krzyzewski.

In the days following the final, Knight called Krzyzewski several times to make sure he was okay. Krzyzewski was fine. He was far better equipped to deal with a crushing loss than his mentor was.

In fact, Knight was still brooding about the Cleveland State loss in Dallas. When a friend asked him why he wasn't going to the NABC banquet, Knight answered, "I'm laying low. I'm kind of struggling right now."

Why?

"Our team just isn't very good."

But, it was pointed out, he had done all that could be done, squeezed all there was to squeeze for twenty-seven games.

"But we played twenty-nine."

Knight paused. Then he added, "And Daryl Thomas is still a pussy. I don't know what to do about him."

So there it was. To Knight, the epitaph for 1985–86 was that Daryl Thomas was still a pussy and Indiana had lost two games in embarrassing fashion. Undoubtedly, that would pop into his mind again and again during fall practice, after first bad half, after the first loss. . . .

The key for Bob Knight remains the same: He is as brilliant a coach as there is. He is an extraordinarily compassionate, caring, sensitive person. No one has ever had a better or more loyal friend. And yet everyone who cares about him remains concerned about his ability to hurt and to cause pain. And the person he hurts most often is Bob Knight.

People around him—friends, coaches, players—want, like Isiah Thomas, to hug him and tell him that they love him. Yet he shies away from that, often acting as if he doesn't think himself worthy of that kind of feeling and then going out and doing something to prove it.

He has won 438 games as a coach, and if he were to coach another twenty years, he could well break Adolph Rupp's all-time record of 880 victories. There is no reason for him not to coach another twenty years. He loves the game, the challenges, and the players. And yet, he still remains unhappy so much of the time. Losses destroy him, and when they do he seems to feel obligated to make everyone and everything around him as miserable as he is. Often, he succeeds.

If only he could let go of things: losses, grudges, tantrums. He is rich and he is famous. In a good mood, there is no one in the world more delightful to be around because he is so bright, so well-read. In a bad mood, there is no one worse. Just as he sees everything in black-and-white terms, he, too, is black and white. Bob Knight never has an average day.

In 1985–86, he saw firsthand what patience could do for a basketball team. He found that he did not have to make a major issue of each defeat in order to get his team to bounce back. He found that if he made the effort, he could control his temper. One can only hope that he will remember these lessons and use them.

He has so much to give—and has given so much. And when he begins his twenty-second season as a college basketball coach this fall, he will only be forty-six years old. A young man with a bright future. If he doesn't destroy it.

Bob Cousy with John Devaney

"Winning and Losing" *From* The Killer Instinct

It was April 1963. I had just arrived in Los Angeles with the Boston Celtics for the final game of the National Basketball Association championship playoffs. After thirteen years with the Celtics this would be my last game.

I walked into my hotel room and locked the door. For the next thirty-six hours I stayed inside that locked room alone. I ordered all my meals sent up. I talked to no one. I didn't answer the telephone. I thought so long and so intensely about Frank Selvy, the Laker guard I would be playing against, that if he had walked into that room I might have leaped at his throat and tried to strangle him. If anyone had touched me or even talked to me, I might have tried to kill him. Or, more likely, I would have broken down and wept.

The next day I ran onto the court to play for that championship with my insides as taut as violin strings, my throat too tight for speaking. Yet outwardly I appeared to be calm, almost daydreamy. My body was under rein, ready to function.

This state—controlled on the outside, emotions erupting inside me—was my most important asset as a competitor. I could be like that, I believed, because I inherited two contrasting personalities. My father was as low-keyed and complacent as you can get. My mother is an emotional, very high-strung person. My father gave me self-control in time of stress; my mother, the overdrive to succeed whatever the cost.

I think you will find this dual personality in many successful people in any competitive profession. The obvious prerequisite for success in competition is an abundance of talent. But as you rise to higher levels you compete against other people who are equally talented. Then you need intensity, a killer instinct that impels you to keep going the extra mile to reach a goal when others slow down or stop.

On a basketball court I had that instinct. I would climb over anyone or anything to succeed, whatever the cost to me or anyone else. Some years ago I was playing in an ordinary three-on-three half-court game at my basketball camp for boys in New Hampshire. One of the players was a boy from Colgate named Duffy, who worked for me as a counselor at the camp. Everyone liked him—he was a decent, nice young man.

Well, we were banging around under the hoop and he made contact with me. I went wild. I flung an elbow into his face. He fell to the ground but he still had a grip on the ball. As if I hadn't done enough, I went right after him and stole the ball. And while I was jerking the ball away, I kicked him in the face—not intentionally, but not accidentally, either. Blood poured from a cut above his eye.

I didn't even stop playing. Someone else took the kid's place while I went on doing my thing out there, playing better now because of the anger he had aroused.

As soon as the game ended, what I hope is my basic nature came to the fore. I felt terrible. I went to the infirmary and spent about an hour with Duffy, telling him how bad I felt.

Yet I knew I would do the same thing again in the heat of competition. In fact, even during meaningless regular-season games I hoped that someone would knock me down, because I played better when I was angry. I believe that if I had never had this killer instinct, this inner drive to keep going when others slowed down, I would have been just another of those six-foot guards who wander briefly into the NBA and then disappear without a trace.

We won that game against the Lakers for the National Basketball Association championship, the fifth in a row for the Boston Celtics. After that game I retired. I was thirty-five and I could have played for another year or two. But I had always wanted to retire when the Celtics and I were on top.

I was well prepared to leave basketball. I had signed contracts with three companies to do public relations and sales work. I was the partner in an insurance company in Worcester, Massachusetts, where I lived with my wife Missie and our two daughters. I had come to Worcester eighteen years earlier, as a freshman at Holy Cross, and had lived there ever since.

But I didn't want to leave basketball. For one thing, it's

only natural to love something you do well. And I had learned from working at my camp that I enjoyed teaching the game to young players. There was more to it than that, though. Looking back, I realize that I was reluctant to give up competition. I had honed my life to a competitive edge, and now, if I couldn't compete myself, I could at least compete through the team I coached.

So when Boston College offered me the position of basketball coach, I thought: *Exactly what I want to do.* The job would keep my hand in the game yet would last only from September to March, leaving me time for my other commitments. And I would be close to home. BC's campus at Chestnut Hill is only an hour's drive from Worcester.

Like many men dedicated to a career, I had been able to give little time to being a family man. From the day I came out of college, I had been wrapped up in my career: traveling with the Celtics during the season, keeping myself prepared physically and mentally, doing all the things that seem to be required of sports celebrities. I had not had the hours to devote to my wife and daughters, who were by this time almost teenagers. Now I thought I could be home with them more often without leaving basketball altogether.

As a coach I had high hopes that the Cousy name would attract the kind of player I wanted—poor and as hungry to succeed as I had been. I grew up in a poor neighborhood on New York's East Side and moved to Queens when I was twelve. There I played schoolyard basketball on the twin principles that you gave it back "in spades" to anybody who gave it to you and that every loose ball was mine.

In my years at BC we tried to develop that kind of player. These young men received a basketball education and a good college education, as well. And in the process I got an education, too.

I experienced the many pressures that most college coaches (and others in competitive businesses) must cope with. The biggest pressure of all was to win games. Though some of the pressure came from others, much of it I put on myself. But there were other conflicting demands—demands that you be honest with your players, that you live within the rules governing college basketball and that you hold on to your own sense of right and wrong. I learned that there were some situations where my killer instinct conflicted with my need to stay honest. And I came to see for the first time that winning might not always mean success and happiness. I had always assumed that winning *was* success.

David Halberstam

From The Breaks of the Game

The key to the Celtic resurgence . . . was the decision to draft Larry Bird. Bird was a player of exceptional potential and many pro scouts lusted after him; he had huge hands and even more remarkable court vision. By a fluke he was eligible for the draft after his junior year even though he made it clear that he planned to return and play one more year of college basketball. That scared off most other general managers. Five other teams eager for immediate help passed on him, but Auerbach, believing that a big forward who could pass as Bird did was the rarest thing in basketball, drafted him. Then he waited a year to negotiate. That meant Bird, far more than the average player, had leverage. He was white, he was an exciting player, and he could sign with the Celtics. Or he could wait a few weeks and be included in the 1979 draft. He would not miss a single game if he did. That put extra pressure on Auerbach. There he was with a floundering franchise, and a shot at a player of rare ability, the kind who comes into the league every four or five years. Because Bird was a country boy, a group of businessmen in Terre Haute helped him pick an agent, and finally decided on Bob Woolf. Woolf was well equipped to do battle with Auerbach; he was as quick to go to the media with moral outrage as Auerbach was. Besides, a precious commodity was at stake. Not surprisingly, in the Bird negotiations Auerbach seemed muted. The bellows and screams of the past became light squeals. There was talk about the fact that the Celtics would not pay any new player, let alone a rookie, more than existing stars. In the end Auerbach gracefully accommodated to the modern era. Bird signed for about $650,000 a year, more than any veteran on the team, more than any Celtic had ever gotten. In 1979 the Boston Celtics, once the tightest of teams, began the season with a payroll of $2,651,071, the highest in the league. The world had indeed changed.

Bird was the rarest kind of media player, someone even better than advertised. Every player on the Celtics improved when he was on the court. "I would never have retired," the thirty-nine-year-old Havlicek told Bob Ryan of the Boston *Globe*, "if I had known there was a chance to play with someone like him." His sense of the court was absolute. He seemed to know where every player was at every moment. Bill Fitch, the new Celtic coach, called him Kodak because of his ability to photograph the court mentally. He was, with that eyesight and those huge hands, perhaps the best passer ever to play forward. If a teammate got free, the ball came to him. Though he was a seemingly limited player physically, with a body that was weak by NBA standards, and had limited flex in his feet (which made him run up and down the court like an elderly woman) he was nevertheless one of the league's top rebounders. He simply compensated for his lack of physical gifts by rare anticipation of where the ball was going. He was a shy, awkward, introverted young man at heart. A cutter just like the Indiana kids in the movie *Breaking Away*, said Bob Ryan. Ryan, one of the keepers of the Celtic flame, had immediately welcomed him as the purest of Celtics and began to promote him, not just for Rookie of the Year, but for Most Valuable Player as well. Though his salary and his skills meant that he was celebrated in the media, he was uncomfortable with his fame. He was clumsy socially, a country boy suddenly let loose in a slick high-powered world. A stranger spotted him riding an elevator to his room in Phoenix and very politely congratulated him on having so successful a rookie season. Bird immediately turned his back, as if to get as far from the man as he could. He hated in particular the pressure of the media, whose representatives were quick and verbal and sure of their words, all the things which he was not. The more he showed up on television the more he was sure it strained his relations with his teammates. That was where his true covenant lay. He was good with them and comfortable with them, because they were linked by the one thing in life he was sure of and comfortable with, basketball. He had, as a good Hoosier boy, tried Indiana University but it was too large for so simple a boy and he had quickly withdrawn. He had for a time worked as a garbage collector. Somewhere in his past there was a brief marriage and a child, and then a separation. Then he had returned to college and played at Indiana State, a more rural college than Indiana. His entrance into the pro league had surprised most professionals. They thought the skills were there but that the body might undo him. Instead his sense of the game and love of the game had served him well. The better the level of the play, the better he was. The Celtics, a dreary team the year before, were a championship contender overnight. All it took was dealing with the right agents and paying $650,000 a year.

Dave Anderson

"Good-by to Jerry West"

When he retires, as it appears he will soon, Jerry West deserves a timepiece that tells only the seconds, not the minutes or the hours.

Through his 14 seasons in the National Basketball Association, he invariably has been at his best in the final seconds when one shot made the difference in the game. He took the one shot. He wanted to take it. His teammates on the Los Angeles Lakers wanted him to take it. During the 1970 championship playoff with the New York Knicks, he made a shot from beyond midcourt with three seconds remaining that tied the score. That's the one shot people remember best. But just as the Knicks won that game in overtime, that shot was a fluke. Jerry West took the one shot in dozens of other games when the situation demanded more skill and poise. That's the way to remember Jerry West, for his consistency in the final seconds when those dozens of other games were decided.

Still vivid is the memory of a Madison Square Garden game when one of the Knicks was about to shoot a foul. West was out near midcourt but Dick Barnett, who was covering him, was keeping his right hand on West's left hip. The ball wasn't even in play yet but Barnett was preparing for the moment he knew would occur if the Lakers got the ball. After the foul shot, that moment arrived.

Jerry West dribbled up court with his right hand. With his left he was slapping away Barnett's pawing hand. West knew he was about to shoot and Barnett knew it. Suddenly, despite Barnett's tenacious defense, West stopped near the foul circle and floated high in the air. His 6-foot-3-inch, 185-pound body was arched perfectly. His left hand was guiding the ball into his right hand. His shot, as it always did when he was shooting well, hit the back of the orange rim and dropped through the basket, hardly touching the net. Jerry West had won another game in the final seconds.

"If it comes down to one shot," he once said, "I like to shoot the ball. I don't worry about it. If it doesn't go in, it doesn't go in."

More often than not, it went in. But he claims that he never aimed at the back rim, that he merely aimed at the basket itself.

"I don't think you have to see very much of the basket to be a good shooter," he was saying recently. "There are a lot of ways of being a good shooter. You," and he shook his fingers, "need these."

But not even Jerry West can shoot from the bench. That's where he'll be when the Lakers oppose the Knicks in Los Angeles tonight.

He's waiting for an abdominal muscle to heal. It might

not heal in time for him to play again. In two weeks, the N.B.A. playoffs will be under way. Even if the Lakers qualify, he might not be able to rejoin them unless they somehow upset the Milwaukee Bucks in their opening series. Without him, that's unlikely. He keeps saying his plans for next season are "indefinite." But that's a word a ballplayer often uses when he isn't ready to acknowledge that he's retiring. He'll never know if the muscle injury was influenced by his long holdout last year.

"That," he said sharply, "is too difficult to even speculate on at this time."

He's 35 years old now. His nose looks 70 years old. His nose has been broken nine times.

"With my different noses," he often jokes, "my wife's been married to nine different guys."

When he retires, he'll undergo surgery to straighten his nose. That nose got busted when he was going for a loose ball or trying for a steal. If the N.B.A. had been keeping statistics on steals when he came out of West Virginia, as they are this season, he probably would be the career leader. As a scorer, he's third on the career list with a 27.3 point average, behind Wilt Chamberlain and Elgin Baylor, two former Laker teammates.

"Of all the things I've done individually," he said when he accumulated 25,000 points early this season, "this is the one thing I'm most proud of. It indicates two things—a long career and a good one."

When the Lakers were here last night, he had on his purple-and-gold satin sweatsuit, but he never took it off. In the warmup, the abdominal muscle wouldn't let him jump. His shots still hit the back rim and dropped straight through but his white sneakers never left the floor. Before the game, he was accorded a special introduction that produced a standing ovation. When the game ended, the Garden fans near the entrance to the locker rooms ignored the other Laker players.

"Jerry, Jerry," they called. "Jerry, Jerry."

It was their way of saying good-by. He'll surely be a coach or a TV analyst but it won't be quite the same.

"When you've been a big kid so many years," he agrees, "it's tough to go out and find something else to do."

Especially in the last few seconds of a game.

John McPhee

Coliseum Hour

We spent an hour at the recent Sport and Camping Show in the New York Coliseum.

Oscar Robertson, of basketball's Cincinnati Royals, entered the hall and was immediately surrounded by at least two thousand people, more than half of them adults. To get near him, they climbed over booths, broke down barricades, and temporarily paralyzed most of the exhibits in the show. National Shoes had engaged Robertson to make an appearance and sign autographs. Cut off by the multitude, we climbed a set of back stairs and found a vantage point on a high mezzanine from which the whole of the main hall was visible. Robertson was now standing in a small "basketball court"—ten feet wide by twenty feet long—between a pair of backboards made of thin composition board and equipped with attached hoops of the sort that are sold in five-and-tens. The crowd—extending from the National Trailways exhibit, in the west, to the Schmidt beer garden, in the east, and from the Golf-o-Tron, in the north, to the pool tables, in the south—seemed to surge like a throng in St. Peter's Square. A little boy, perhaps ten years old, stood beside Robertson, and Robertson handed him a basketball. The boy took a shot, and missed. Robertson retrieved the ball and handed it to him again. The boy shot again, and missed. Robertson leaned down and talked to the boy. Not just a word or two. He spoke into the boy's ear for half a minute. The boy shot again. Swish. Robertson himself seemed reluctant to try a shot. The baskets were terrible, and—even if they had not been—a basketball player makes only about half his shots anyway. A few misses, and this crowd really would not have understood. Moreover, Robertson was wearing an ordinary suit, so his movements would be restricted. He signed a few autographs. "Shoot, Big O!" someone called out. Others took up the cry. "Shoot, Big O!" Robertson turned aside and signed another autograph. "Shoot, Big O!" Robertson studied one of the baskets. This might have been a mistake, because there was no retreating now. Once a basketball player, with a ball in his hand, looks up at a basket, almost nothing can make him resist the temptation to take a shot. Robertson stepped back to a point about seventeen feet from the basket and lifted the ball high, and a long set shot rolled off his fingers and began to arc toward the basket with a slow backspin. The crowd was suddenly quiet. Everybody watched the ball except Robertson, whose eyes never left the basket until the ball had dropped in. He shot again. Swish. Again. Swish. Five, six, seven in a row. There was no one else in the Coliseum now. Robertson—making set shots, jump shots, even long, graceful hook shots—had retreated from the crowd into the refuge of his talent.

Bob Ryan and Terry Pluto

From Forty-Eight Minutes

Larry Bird is not as good a shooter now as he was in college. The general public is unaware that Larry Bird goes around sinking shots like the one he has just made with 40 percent of his fingers on his shooting hand a mess.

Bird has to play professional basketball with a badly mangled right index finger and a permanently bent and dislocated right pinky. Since becoming a Celtic, he has had to reconstruct his shot in order to overcome his—there really is no other word—*deformities*.

In the spring of his senior year at Indiana State, Bird, a big baseball fan, was playing a pick-up softball game. He was in left field when his brother Mike hit a line drive in his direction. Bird, being as orthodox in baseball as he is in basketball, eschewed the fancy one-hand catch. He did it by the book, bringing his open right hand in to close the glove as he caught the ball. But he got his hand in too soon and the ball smashed into the index finger.

Two operations later, he was left with the finger he has now. It is swollen and bent. He cannot make a fist with his right hand. Celtics team physician Dr. Thomas Silva once described the break in Bird's right index finger in terms of the difference between snapping a pencil in half and having someone smash it with a hammer. Bird's right index finger was smashed with the hammer.

How traumatic was this for Larry Bird? Only he knows. He never brings up the finger in public, never curses his misfortune and never allows any prolonged discussion of the finger. To him, it is something that happened, and something he has learned to deal with.

He was very concerned about the finger when he first signed with the Celtics. Throughout both the weeklong rookie camp in August 1979 and the entire training camp that year, he played with the injured finger heavily taped to his middle finger. He was very fearful of having the finger bumped or hyperextended.

On opening night he took the floor against the Houston Rockets with the same taping arrangement. He scored fourteen points on six-for-twelve shooting. He tried an experiment the following evening in the Richfield Coliseum against Cleveland. Rather than taping the index finger and middle finger together from top to bottom, he simply taped the fingers loosely above the joint, thus allowing himself more flexibility. He shot twelve for seventeen and scored twenty-eight points.

He maintained this arrangement for the next nine games. On the night of November 9, 1979, a home game against the Kansas City Kings, he again started the ballgame with the fingers loosely taped. But when he emerged from the locker room after intermission, the tape was gone. He finished the game with seventeen points on six-for-eleven shooting. He did make the game's key basket, but it was a left-handed jump hook.

Afterward he explained what prompted him to tear off the tape—forever. "I decided I had to stop babying myself," he declared. "If it gets bumped, it gets bumped."

But he does wear tape every night on the pinky. That finger has been so continually mauled that it now is permanently crooked. Bird has devised a taping method to protect the finger, while allowing it sufficient mobility for shooting and passing purposes. Compared to the gravity of the damaged right index finger, his injured right pinky can be classified as a mere annoyance.

The fact remains that Larry Bird has adjusted to an injury that could easily have ruined the career of a less tough-minded person. The two most important fingers for a shooter are the index finger and the middle finger. The ball rolls off these two digits, and Bird has had to compensate for a whole new feel. Bird has put in the time to remake his shot because he is a man of uncommon resolve. The adjustment has clearly been ongoing: From a shooting percentage of .474 as a rookie Bird gradually improved to a career-high of .522 in the 1984–85 season. His three-point accuracy has likewise gone upward.

Bird has occasionally made reference to his shooting prowess as a collegian, as opposed to the way he is now. As great a shooter as he is, there is absolutely no doubt he would have been substantially better as a professional had he never damaged that right index finger. This is not a sufficiently comforting thought for the rest of the NBA.

Editor's note: William Goldman, in *Wait Till Next Year*, quotes Bird as saying, "In the summers, I'll try and see how many free throws I can make in a row. Summer before last I broke a hundred, I hit a hundred and five. This past summer I got up to a hundred and sixty-three. Now, when I go to the line I figure, 'If I can hit a hundred and sixty-three in a row, I can make these two.' Next summer I plan on going past a hundred and sixty-three."

~

Part dump, part shrine, part House of Horrors, part House of Basketball Worship, the Boston Garden is a singular stop on the NBA tour. The only existing NBA venue anywhere near the Garden's age is Chicago Stadium, six years its junior, but the true mystique in Chicago is all wrapped up in the resident hockey team, not the basketball team.

With the sixteen championship banners and the two sheafs of retired numbers hanging down from the rafters, the Garden has an aura no other NBA arena can match. Visitors are not merely playing a basketball game when they come to Boston. They are more like guests who have been invited over for tea. The banners serve as draperies in this spacious living room. The Celtics and their fans act as if it is a *privilege* to play there. The apparent responsibility of the visiting squad is to provide a certain amount of competition, but only enough to allow the Boston players a proper showcase for a display of basketball expertise.

The business of the Boston Garden on nights when the Celtics play is basketball, and nothing else. There is no rock music blaring from the loudspeakers (given the wretched quality of the sound system, this is even more of a blessing than the most diehard traditionalist might think). There are no cheerleaders. Public address announcer Andrew Jick does not introduce the team as *"Your"* Boston Celtics, the way so many obnoxious PA men are forced to do around the league. There are, thank God, no mascots.

There is only basketball, and it's played on the hallowed parquet floor. It is basketball as it existed ten, twenty, thirty, and forty years ago. The Boston Garden has had new seats and a new scoreboard installed in recent years, but it's still sitting atop a train station, it's still reached by a screeching overhead transit system, and it's still got the same feel it had when the best player on the team was Ed Sadowski or Fat Freddy Scolari. A fan whose last game here was in 1950 wouldn't feel out of place. He'd just have more company.

The Garden isn't the noisiest building. It is neither the biggest nor the smallest NBA arena. It is, however, one of the more intimate ones. Built in 1928 with ice hockey, indoor track, and boxing in mind, it is more a high-rise than a sloping-back arena. It is said to be a scaled-down version of the famed Madison Square Garden that was located on Fiftieth Street and Eighth Avenue in New York, and, in fact, the official name of the eating and drinking establishment housed inside is the "Boston Madison Square Garden Club."

For years the capacity for basketball at the Garden was 13,909. The number passed into the Bostonian vocabulary as a standard of reference. A man would come back from ten-o'clock Mass on Sunday morning and say to his neighbor, "Geez. Thirteen nine-oh-nine at St. Bartholomew's today." A man would come back to his desk after visiting the company cafeteria and say to his fellow worker, "Watch out. It's thirteen nine-oh-nine up there."

The interesting thing about the 13,909 was that very seldom during any regular-season Celtics game from 1946 to 1972 were that many people actually in the building. There is a great deal of talk about how Bob Cousy saved professional basketball in the town, but it's not as if he made basketball a religion in Boston. Attendance improved from an average of 4,252 a game in 1949–50 to 6,184 the following year, Cousy's first. In the next five years prior to the advent of Bill Russell the largest per-game average in Boston was 8,064 in 1955–56.

People from the outside have never understood that basketball was very much a novelty in Boston back in those days. Wintertime in Boston meant one thing: hockey. The Bruins, not the Celtics, were the team with tradition. The city of Boston was so uninterested in basketball that the sport was not included in the school system's roster of sporting activities for two decades, starting in the mid-twenties. The suburbs, yes; the city, no.

Boston's very presence as a charter member of the Basketball Association of America (the forerunner of the NBA) came about simply because Walter Brown thought it might be a good business proposition. Brown ran the Boston Garden, and his objective, shared by the preponderance of BAA owners, was to fill some dates in his arena on nights when there was no hockey, boxing, wrestling, or indoor track. There was no great clamor for a professional basketball team in Boston in 1946.

Brown was not a wealthy man. He was a sportsman, a gentleman, and a man of honor. Though his entire sports background was in hockey, he grew to love his Celtics as if they were his own offspring. He believed in them, for reasons that were not terribly apparent at the box office.

Truly modern professional basketball came to Boston in 1950 when Brown hired a brash Brooklynite named Arnold J. (Red) Auerbach to coach his team. Auerbach had already coached two professional teams. He was the first coach of the Washington Capitols in 1946, and he had been the coach of the Tri-Cities Hawks in 1949–50. Auerbach was opinionated and autocratic. Walter Brown knew next to nothing about basketball, which was fine with Auerbach; Red liked the idea of running the entire basketball operation.

Auerbach quickly discovered that he had come to a basketball wasteland. The local newspapers had only marginal interest in the team and the entire sport of professional basketball. One paper, the *Boston Post*, refused to cover the team at all for the first few years. There was great fervor in Boston concerning college basketball, however, the hook being a classy Holy Cross outfit. The Crusaders had won the NCAA title in 1947, and they were the focal point of many highly successful doubleheaders in the Boston Garden over the next three years. The Boston press had particularly embraced Bob Cousy, the flashy Holy Cross guard. Cousy was practically a local demigod, and it made perfect sense to the Boston press that he be made a Celtic. Auerbach, however, was an orthodox basketball man who thought Cousy's unique playing style, which included behind-the-back passes and all sorts of individual gestures, was horrifying. He would rather have given up smoking cigars than draft Bob Cousy. His disgust reached a peak at a writers' luncheon shortly after Auerbach was signed to coach the team. "Am I supposed to win," he inquired, "or please the local yokels?"

The joke was on Auerbach, though, because when the Chicago team that had originally selected Cousy folded and the players were dispersed, Cousy's name was drawn out of a hat by Brown. That's how the man the world would soon know as "Mr. Basketball" became a Boston Celtic.

The Celtics' following was small but loyal, and quite ethnic. The core of their fandom came from the Jewish community of the Greater Boston area, specifically the residents of Brookline, a wealthy enclave almost entirely surrounded by the city of Boston. Sellouts were very infrequent. As an example of Boston's professional basketball consciousness, Brown felt it necessary to secure a preliminary game featuring two Boston high schools the night of the first NBA All-Star Game in 1951.

Auerbach didn't help the situation. He was a coach and general manager, not an impresario. His idea of promotion was to get the schedule printed. His theory was that you opened the doors, they came, they liked the show, and they'd come back. He wasn't about to beg. If you didn't like the product, there was obviously something wrong with you, not him, and certainly not with professional basketball.

The Celtics would have gone under were it not for the fighting spirit of Walter Brown. This amazing man, whose memory remains so sacred that people like Auerbach can hardly mention his name without getting misty, did absolutely everything he could to keep the Celtics alive. This included taking out a second mortgage on his home to help finance the team and reaching into his own bank account to give his players the playoff shares they had earned following one season. The players had cooperated by taking Walter at his word that there would be some cash forthcoming. Imagine anything like that happening today.

The five thousand or so diehards who came every night in the early fifties grew to appreciate basketball as much as any other group of fans in the league. Some of them, men such as Harold Furash, who had attended the very first Celtics practice in 1946 and who remains a season-ticket holder today, became friendly with the players and management. They were very much a part of the Celtics "family." They could not understand why more people hadn't learned to love professional basketball as they did, but once the game started their only concern was the basketball being played, not the empty seats alongside them.

Walter Brown attempted to solve his attendance problems by playing home games elsewhere. The Celtics played a number of "home" games in nearby Providence. In the 1952–53 season the "Boston" Celtics played twenty-one of their seventy NBA games in Boston. Granted, playing in homes-away-from-home or neutral sites was not an isolated practice in those days, but few teams spent as much time *not* playing in their own home as the Celtics.

The Celtics in those pre-Russell days were perennial bridesmaids, mostly because they lacked a rebounder to get them the ball. They had a fine finesse center in "Easy" Ed Macauley, a consummate jump shooter in Bill Sharman, and the man who set the standard for all playmakers in Cousy. They could score when they got the ball, but they lacked any sort of inside defensive presence, and they were often beaten badly on the backboards.

The first time Red Auerbach saw Bill Russell perform

for the University of San Francisco, he knew that the rangy center was the answer. Russell was a new type of basketball force. The big men who had come before him featured offense. They had hook shots and their prime thrust was scoring. The 6-9 Russell was a substandard (and uninterested) shooter. His skill lay in rebounding and in defense, where he had a novel concept: Someone would throw up a shot, and Russell would block it. This just wasn't done in those days.

But how to get him? The Celtics didn't have a high enough draft pick in 1956. There was no way Russell would last long enough to reach Boston. The only way was to make a trade.

The first pick belonged to the Rochester Royals. Their owner, Lester Harrison, liked Russell, but wasn't sure he wanted to pay him what he'd ask. The bidding competition in that far different sports world was the Harlem Globetrotters; Russell did have financial leverage. Harrison decided he wouldn't take Russell, and, anyway, he was quite pleased to select Duquesne's Sihugo Green, a superb 6-3 athlete.

Next up was St. Louis. They were owned by a fiery fellow named Ben Kerner. He and Auerbach had been owner and coach, once upon a time, back when the franchise was located in the Tri-Cities of Moline and Davenport, Iowa, and Rock Island, Illinois. Kerner had fired Auerbach. Kerner wasn't sure how well a big black man would go over in St. Louis.

Kerner was amenable to a trade. The deal was this: Macauley and the rights to Kentucky All-American Cliff Hagan (then coming out of the service) for the rights to Russell. Auerbach really hated to trade Macauley, whom he loved dearly, but Macauley said it was all right because he had a sick child, and he came from St. Louis, so it would be a good move for him to go back home. If his playing skill weren't enough, his graciousness at a time of Celtics need would have been enough for Auerbach to get Ed's number 22 retired and hoisted to the Garden ceiling.

The Russell era actually began in December 1956, because he was busy helping the United States win the Olympic gold medal in basketball down in Melbourne, Australia. When he joined the Celtics they were already in first place with a 16–8 record, in large measure due to the contributions of another rookie, Tom Heinsohn. Auerbach had acquired the 6-7 forward via a device known as the "territorial draft choice," which gave each NBA team natural rights to players attending schools within a certain geographic radius. Heinsohn had gone to Holy Cross, about forty-five miles west of the Boston Garden as the crow flies.

Russell immediately acclimated himself to the NBA. But by the time he retired thirteen years later, the league had yet to acclimate itself to him. The Celtics won their first championship on April 13, 1957, defeating the St. Louis Hawks by a 125–123 score in double overtime. They did so before a roaring crowd of, yes, 13,909. It was the first of eleven championships in the Russell era.

Curiously, this was one of only two seasons in which they averaged as many as ten thousand people a game in Russell's time. There have been innumerable theories concerning the low regular-season attendance figures over the next dozen years. One of the most prevalent beliefs was that the Celtics were so good, so *overwhelming*, that people were simply bored. Supporters of that theory point to the fact that the only other season in the Russell era in which the Celtics averaged over ten thousand was 1965–66, when the Celtics lost the Eastern Division regular-season title for the first time since 1955–56, finishing second to Philadelphia by one game. See, they said. People want competition.

There was a lot more to the Boston attendance situation than the lack of good pennant races, however. Start with the Boston Bruins. They may have been infrequent challengers for the Stanley Cup (1941 was their last triumph), but they still pulled in big crowds. As the years went on it became fashionable to follow the Celtics during the playoffs, but the night-in, night-out support was disappointingly limited.

Media coverage was inadequate. None of the Boston papers covered the team on the road until the playoffs. The papers would cover the road games by listening to the radio broadcasts and writing stories based on the colorful and, shall we say, somewhat slanted descriptions of renowned Celtics announcer Johnny Most. It can be argued that skimpy coverage led to uninformed and, ultimately, uninterested fans.

The Celtics gradually became more and more beloved as time went on. People traveling outside Boston learned that the rest of the nation thought the Celtics were something special. People in Ames, Iowa, or Tucumcari, New Mexico, who occasionally got to see the Celtics on television assumed that the Celtics were a hot item locally. In truth they were honored with lip service but basically ignored until special moments, much like another underappreciated Boston treasure, the *Christian Science Monitor.*

Very little of this academic appreciation of the Celtics as a civic bellwether was reflected in the box office. The true believers kept coming, however, and their ranks grew slightly during the Russell years. The pinnacle for these loyal fans came in 1969, when an aging band of Celtics, who had finished a distant fourth during the regular season in the Eastern Division, won successive series over Philadelphia, New York, and Los Angeles to win the eleventh title in thirteen years.

Russell retired that summer, ending one of the great careers in American athletic history. He had played thirteen years and had won eleven championships. He was the only constant on those eleven champions, save Auerbach, of course. Russell had even coached the last two title squads following Auerbach's 1966 retirement from the bench to the front office. With typical Auerbach logic, he had deduced that Russell wouldn't play for anyone else but Russell, so he made him coach. That Russell happened to be the first black coach in one of the four major sports leagues made Auerbach's decision a sociology story as well.

Life without Bill (and without the brilliant Sam Jones) was rocky. The 1969–70 Celtics were impotent in the middle, finishing sixth in a seven-team division. Attendance dropped over 1,400 people a game, to 7,504. There were no sellouts, and the largest crowd of the season came on opening night. The diehards came to cheer for old favorites John Havlicek and Don Nelson, while wondering if they'd ever again enjoy basketball as much without Bill Russell out there blocking shots and igniting fast breaks.

The wait was brief, because in the 1970 draft Auerbach, picking fourth, chose a 6–foot–9 redheaded backboard eater named Dave Cowens. Red wasn't sure exactly what Cowens was (some teams thought he was a forward, others a center); he just knew that Cowens was fast, strong, smart, and as competitive as anyone he had ever encountered and that he could go get the basketball. Sound familiar?

With Cowens in the middle, a thirty-year-old Havlicek

playing the king on the Celtics' chessboard, Nelson popping in his soft jumpers, and a young tandem of Jo Jo White and Don Chaney providing the team with some much-needed athleticism in the backcourt, the Celtics brought life back to the Garden. Attendance rose slightly in 1970–71, a little more the next season, and then spilled over the magic ten thousand mark in the '72–73 season, when the Celtics won sixty-eight games and missed winning a championship, they believed, only because Havlicek suffered a shoulder separation during the Eastern Conference finals against New York.

Most Celticologists of the times believed that ten thousand was an optimum figure. Concurrent with the rise of the Celtics was the ascension of the Boston Bruins to an all-time peak of popularity. These were the big, bad bruins of Phil Esposito, Ken Hodge, Johnny (Pie) McKenzie, Derek (Turk) Sanderson, Gerry Cheevers, and especially Bobby Orr, the wonderchild defenseman. They owned the town as no athletic team had since the Red Sox of the teens. The Celtics were doing all right, but compared to the Bruins they were a Double A franchise. In the spring of 1973, it was impossible to imagine the Bruins would ever be anything but number one in the winter and the Celtics would ever be anything but number two.

But what did account for the Celtics' appeal? Why were the basketball fans more willing to come see this team than the hallowed Russell teams? No one knew for sure, but there was no shortage of theories:

1. Russell was personally unapproachable, whereas Cowens was an accessible superstar, a real workingman's hero.
2. The Celtics were now attracting second-generation fans

for the first time. The children of the original fans now had their own money to spend. They were attracted to the Celtics as kids and now they were consumers. Plus, Dad and Uncle Sid were still around, so everyone went together.

3. Media coverage was more extensive. The Boston papers had expanded their coverage. The Celtics had good local television coverage. Johnny Most was now a certified local legend, and it was chic to listen to his hysterical accounts of the games.
4. The Celtics featured white stars. This last subject is endlessly debated in Boston, a city where race is a very volatile topic. Auerbach was a pioneer in sports, drafting and signing the first black in the NBA (Chuck Cooper, 1950), becoming one of the first two coaches to start five black players (both the '65–66 Celtics and 76ers did so), and hiring the first black coach (Russell) in the NBA. In addition, he insisted on black-white roommate pairs whenever possible. In terms of his personal record, the Celtics stood above reproach when it came to fostering the rise of black players in the NBA.

But while the NBA was getting blacker and blacker, the Celtics were able to hold on to some superior white players. Cowens, with his flaming red hair, was a vivid contrast to Russell. Could the Celtics help it if a particular fan felt more empathy toward Cowens than Russell? Havlicek was white. Nelson was white. Paul Westphal, another exciting white player, joined the team in 1972. The Celtics clearly maintained their appeal in the seventies for the biased consumer. Only a fool would fail to understand that. The question was whether or not the Celtics have ever pandered to the bigots who happened to be basketball fans. The Celtics maintained then, and maintain now, that they don't.

Rival general managers and owners envied the Celtics for their good fortune, as they defined it. Blacks were taking over the game on the court, and the Celtics appeared to be the only team capable of winning a high percentage of games while still employing a large number of white players. The professionals found it difficult to criticize the Celtics when they would gladly have traded half their team to get their hands on a Dave Cowens or a John Havlicek, players who might have induced the same white fans who were staying home in their own cities to come out to the games.

The NBA existed in a frighteningly racist society, and few doubted that one reason why the NBA had not attained the stature it deserved was that large segments of white America didn't want to patronize a sport featuring so many blacks. The flip side of this was that the blacks who would ostensibly love to come watch their own heroes simply could not afford tickets.

The Celtics won championships with Cowens at center and Havlicek playing a major role in both 1974 and 1976. These championships meant a great deal to Auerbach, who wanted to show the world that the Celtics could accomplish great things even without Russell. The Celtics had clearly broadened their fan base by now, and they silently cheered when the Bruins and Bobby Orr (by then the owner of two battered knees) had an acrimonious parting in 1976. The Bruins have never recovered from his departure.

But very little went right for the Celtics in the next few years, on and off the court. Cowens took a "leave of absence" after the eighth game of the 1977 season. He returned two months later, and the Celtics were able to extend the Philadelphia 76ers to a seventh game the following spring, but the fabric of the team had been irrevocably damaged. The team won thirty games in '77–78, and the highlight of the season came on the final day of an otherwise dreary year, when a capacity crowd came to bid a teary farewell to thirty-seven-year-old John Havlicek.

Public faith in the Celtics had eroded, although the actual attendance figures could have been worse. From a high of 13,446 in the '75–76 season, the Celtics' average slipped to 10,193 in '78–79, when the only sellout of the season came on opening night. The Cavaliers handled them by fourteen points, and a lot of people said good-bye to the Celtics for the season.

By this time the team was in the hands of John Y. Brown (no relation to Walter), a mercurial Kentucky blowhard who had so alienated Auerbach that the cigar smoker had seriously considered accepting an offer to take over operation of the Knicks, of all people. The Celtics had gone through seven ownership regimes following the sudden death of Walter Brown in the fall of 1964, but all interested parties consider the meddlesome Brown to have been the worst of the lot.

His most egregious act came on February 14, 1979, when, without Auerbach's knowledge or approval, he took three precious number-one draft picks Auerbach had been hoarding and shipped them to New York for the skittish Bob McAdoo, a three-time NBA scoring champion whose style and personality had no chance of fitting in with the Celtics, even a Celtics team as unrecognizable as that one.

Auerbach has never forgotten or forgiven. Years later, he

told an interviewer with regard to John Y. Brown: ". . . and he'd make deals. Well, he made one great big deal that could have destroyed the team, without even consulting me. . . . He did ruin it. We just happened to put it back together again, luckily. One wrong guy can ruin it so fast your head will swim."

Auerbach's outlook brightened considerably when Brown's partner bought him out following the 1978–79 season. Harry Mangurian, in contrast to his bombastic business partner, was from the "speak softly and carry a big stick" school. He was a tough man on the inside, but he kept a very low public profile. And he wasn't foolish enough to make deals without consulting Red Auerbach.

At the conclusion of the 1979–80 season, the Celtics needed to do two things. They needed a coach, and they needed to restore public confidence. Auerbach found his coach in Bill Fitch, who had just resigned after nine successful years in Cleveland. And there was a way to restore public confidence. All the Celtics had to do was sign Larry Bird to a contract.

Auerbach had drafted Bird the previous spring. The Celtics had two high draft choices, number six and number eight. He took Bird, who had a year of eligibility remaining at Indiana State, at number six. He took Freeman Williams, a scoring machine from Portland State, at number eight. Williams would never play a game for the Celtics before being included in a controversial John Y. Brown-inspired trade with the San Diego Clippers, né the Buffalo Braves.

The Celtics had one calendar year to sign Bird, or else he would be thrown back into the 1979 draft pool. In the interim, Bird led Indiana State to a 33–1 record and a berth in the national championship game. When Auerbach drafted him, many knowledgeable experts were saying the 6-9 forward from French Lick, Indiana, could become an All-Pro. By the time the Celtics started negotiating with Bob Woolf, Bird's agent, the opinions had been revised upward. The only question appeared to be whether Bird would become the greatest forward of all time, or the greatest player of any description.

Harry Mangurian was not afraid to spend the money. He signed Bird for the highest salary ever paid a rookie in any major professional sport, a sum in excess of $600,000 a year. Since Boston was something of a backwater outpost when it came to college basketball in those days, not everyone knew what to expect. However, the average fan was pleased to know that there was something resembling a savior out there and that the Celtics had not been timid about obtaining him for their very own.

It took Bird something like two months to become the most popular basketball player Boston had ever seen. Bigger individually than Cousy, bigger than Russell, bigger than Havlicek, bigger than Cowens, bigger than anybody. He combined the best skills of each previous Boston basketball superstar, and he possessed a work ethic unsurpassed in the history of the sport. He demonstrated the ability to shoot, pass, rebound, defend, and make clutch plays. He wasn't afraid to take a charge or dive on the floor for a loose ball, things many gifted players in the league believe are actions best left to the low-price overachievers. Boston's basketball fans, weaned on the best basketball teams that had ever been assembled, recognized that their entire experience had been educating them to appreciate this one man, a player so versatile and compelling that he represented a microcosm of everything good the sport has to offer. Of all the gym joints, in all the towns in the world, he had come to theirs. Watching Larry Bird play became a privilege. Dazed basketball aficionados wandered around asking themselves, "What wonderful thing did I ever do to deserve *this*?"

It didn't hurt, of course, that Bird was white.

Would the Celtics' fans have embraced Larry Bird as they did if he were black? If, for example, he were Magic Johnson? Probably not. Would they be so in love with Kevin McHale and his wondrous rejections if he were black? Probably not. Would comparable players with darker skin have created such a passion in this racially fractured city? Probably not. Does this change their basketball accomplishments? *Absolutely not.*

Meanwhile, attendance soared. Forgotten were the days when a good season-ticket total was eight hundred. On December 19, 1980, the Celtics defeated the Houston Rockets by a 133–119 score before 14,570, which was 750 below the then capacity figure of 15,320. Those were the last official empty seats for any Celtics game, regular-season, playoff, or exhibition. The Celtics sell over 12,500 season tickets annually in a building that now seats 14,890 (a renovation that added thirty-two luxury boxes reduced the capacity). The waiting list for season tickets is years long. Following the 1985–86 season the Celtics raised their ticket prices substantially. There were eight season-ticket cancellations.

There were championships in 1981, 1984, and 1986, and a loss in the 1985 championship finals. With each passing year the crowd feels more and more a part of a continuum. There are now third-generation followers, fans to whom Nate Archibald, and not Bob Cousy, represents the Good Old Days. This is the Boston Garden.

William Goldman

"Revolution Comes to Madison Square"
From Wait Till Next Year (with Mike Lupica)

If you're a performer, and your agent calls and tells you he's got it all locked up for you to sing the National Anthem before a Knicks game, a lot of thoughts go through your head. You know it's not a big deal—but then you also know you're not The Boss, filling the Meadowlands with eighty thousand plus. And you know you're not going to get rich—maybe a pair of freebies, maybe a little more.

But it's a job—and a singer's nothing without people to listen. And it's exposure; a lot of media people go to Knick games. Or used to.

The real reason you decide to sing, though, is because, if you're a performer, you know the legends. Lana Turner . . . Lana Turner sitting . . . sitting on a stool in a drug store . . .

Schwab's drug store . . . Lana Turner just *sitting* there at the right time and before you know it, fame, fortune, and Johnny Stompanato were all hers.

Or Shirley the Gypsy. Understudying. And just like in the movies, the star gets sick. So Shirley goes on. And just like in the movies, a big Hollywood producer is in that matinee audience. And he offers her a shot. And she takes it. And thirty-five years after *The Pajama Game,* Shirley MacLaine is still a very famous lady.

So singing the "Star Spangled Banner" at Madison Square Garden before a New York Knickerbocker basketball game may not be a *big* deal. But it's still a deal.

And *ohhhh,* the possibilities.

So you relearn the words and maybe you take an extra voice lesson, and you try to figure what's best in the way of attire, and then the day comes, 7:35 arrives, you're announced as a "famous recording artist," which could mean you may once actually have been inside a studio, and you're on. Standing alone. Mid-court.

Oh, say can you see,
By the dawn's early light . . .

Not bad so far. Not the best you've ever sung, but now you're over your nerves, the fear of getting the words wrong, and you begin to relax.

What so proudly we hailed
At the twilight's last gleaming.
Whose broad stripes and bright stars,
Through the perilous—

"YOU SUCK."

You're standing there and suddenly you find yourself entering a nightmare. Did someone actually think you were so bad they shouted "You suck" in the middle of America's anthem? Could it be true? No. No. Maybe you're not great but you don't *suck*. Sure you've been in better voice but who anywhere does a decent job with this turkey of a song?

But what if that voice was right? What if you do suck? What kind of a future can you have when a stranger who didn't sound drunk could be such a quick and violent critic? Now—

"GO TO HELL."

A different voice. From a different part of the arena. High, high up, this one came from. And that's good and that's bad. Bad because who tells a stranger doing his best to "go to hell"? Good because at least, being high, high up, he can't physically assault you.

And the rocket's red—

"YOU STINK."

Not terrific, this new voice's sentiment, but not as bad maybe as "Go to hell" and a lot better than "You suck." *What's going on at the Garden?*

And finally, finally you understand, as the next malediction comes first from in front of you, then is picked up by another voice to the side. Then a third joins in, all of them going:

"FUCK YOU, HUBIE."

"FUCK YOU, YOU SONOFABITCH, HUBIE."

"HUBEEEE, FOKKKKKKKKKKK YOU!"

They weren't hating you—you can still be the next Sinatra. It was Hubie Brown, the Knick's coach, they were addressing their sentiments toward.

And indeed they were. For the above is a not unreasonable Xerox of what it was like sitting there before a game near the end of Hubie's reign of error.

Hubie Brown gives great press, so for years he was able to fight clear of corners with his remarkable knowledge of basketball statistics. For if any of you have heard him on the networks, you know you are listening to no dummy.

Nor is he a terrible coach. He's just a terrible *professional* coach—I think he'd be sensational in college, where his teaming of knowledge and abuse would work for the four years of a scholarship.

To understand the dental-like pain of sitting through a Hubie Brown–coached team season after season, let me posit two questions:

1. Who would you rather have as your point guard, Magic or Isiah? Tough question, and there is no wrong answer. They are both among the greatest passers in history, Isiah is a better scorer, Magic has his size. My guess would be, because of the Lakers' success and exposure, if you asked a thousand people, Magic would win eight hundred votes.

2. Who would you rather have as your point guard, Magic Johnson or Rory Sparrow? (And no, this is not a shaggy dog story.) Obviously I can't be sure, but as long as I'm making up the poll, I'm going to make up the result. If you asked a thousand people, Magic would win, nine hundred and ninety-nine to one.

Well, Hubie Brown is that one.

Why? Because in the first place, Magic wouldn't take Hubie's shit, the constant insulting, the obvious contempt in which he holds his athletes. (They're all so stupid.) The real reason is this: Sparrow, an absolutely adequate guard, was willing to totally follow orders. To strip himself of creativity of any kind.

This is a totally creative game. If Hubie were casting *Hamlet,* he wouldn't want Olivier, no, give him Maria Ouspenskaya for the lead. She'd be grateful.

Hubie, you must understand, called the Knick plays. I suppose the standard memory of watching Hubie's Knicks would be when the Knicks would get a defensive rebound, kick it out to Sparrow on the break—

—only he wouldn't break. He'd slow, look over at the bench where Hubie would be standing—his right hand in a fist, or his arms crossed at the wrist—signaling the play.

Just like Tom Landry.

The Knick "play"—there was really only one and it consisted of dumping the ball into whichever big man near the basket seemed most open—worked okay when he had a truly great scorer like Bernard King to take the shot. But when Bernard went down, and the other scorers too, Hubie didn't change his system. Same old shitty play only now it was being executed by a CBA refugee.

Agony.

Masterson, my fellow masochist who I attend the games with, had been among the first to go mad. The year before, in a game against Cleveland, he suddenly started shrieking for them to beat us, humiliate us, stomp us mercilessly. "It just came over me," he remembers now, not smiling. "I didn't go to the game intending to root for the damn Cavaliers. But I realized if they destroyed us, and then if *everyone* destroyed us, maybe they'd do something about that asshole."

When the Knicks breezed to four wins in their first sixteen games with the media at last blessedly merciless, Gulf + Western circled the wagons, decided on decapitation: Hubie was gone.

Such joy.

He was replaced by Bob Hill, who did a decent enough job with what he inherited. For Hill was faced with this one weeny problem: Most of the players he inherited from Hubie were ploughhorses—and Hill wanted an up-tempo game, to pitch the shackles, to run. So Hubie was gone, and such wonderful riddance, but the Knicks were now bifurcated. (Just trying to keep you on your toes.)

The fans, thrilled with the enemy banished, began to realize that, banished or not, Hubie's presence was still felt. The Knicks were now just a different shade of horrendous.

Bill Bradley

From Life on the Run

A professional basketball player must be able to run six miles in a game, a hundred games a year—jumping and pivoting under constant physical contact. My body becomes so finely tuned that three days without workouts makes a noticeable difference in timing, wind, and strength. I believe that basketball is the most physically grueling of all professional sports.

Only the athlete himself really knows if he feels well enough for competition. Doctors don't always understand the athlete's healing time schedule. Sometimes I have been told I could play when I knew I couldn't, and sometimes I have been told I couldn't play when I knew I could. I usually consult three doctors when I have a fairly serious injury. After getting their opinions, which often differ, I decide, myself, whether I can play without danger or permanent damage.

Injuries after thirty occur more frequently and they are less responsive to treatment. Top condition is harder to regain and maintain. The real pro is not the twenty-five-year-old who can whip back into shape with two weeks of careless work but the veteran who tests his body each year to see if he still has it, knowing that someday he won't. During the first week of training camp DeBusschere (age 33) went straight home to bed after every workout. The week was equally difficult for me. After running a mile twice a day for three weeks prior to the camp and shooting an hour a day for twenty-one straight days, my body still wasn't ready for the two-a-day workouts under Holzman. The first day my calves felt as if a knife had split them open. My quadriceps the next day went into spasms so that each step felt as if the muscles had been replaced with armored plates. Pain spread to the back of the legs and around the knees. Two days later the back pain began along the sciatic nerve. It was a tiring pain, not sharp, but it felt as if the strands of a string were breaking until only one remained. Then there was the overall fatigue, which only sleep can cure, and there was never enough sleep. Finally, after the first two scrimmages, I realized that four months of normal life had ended, for I was so bruised that when I rolled over in bed I found my body studded with pain.

Teammates often joke about the shape of my body and its limited athletic capabilities. They say I'm the only player in the league with the body of an eighty-year-old man. I am not well-proportioned, and even when I am in peak condition I can't manage relatively simple physical exercises, I can't do twenty push-ups, and I would need a winch to lift most barbells. Standing, legs straight, I can't touch the floor with anything but my feet. With my physical equipment, just playing in the pros is a minor miracle.

Basketball is such a specialized skill that I restrict myself to it exclusively. I don't swim or play tennis, or hike or ride bicycles, or lift weights during the season. Each sport calls upon a different set of muscles and physically I am concerned only about my profession. After each game or practice, ice packs and whirlpools and sometimes anti-inflammatory drugs like endicin or butazolidin save the body for another exertion. A friend likens my body to a jet plane. When it is aloft it can accomplish things with power and speed. When it is on the ground it is helpless, unmaneuverable, and in need of repair. As I sit with my feet in a barrel of ice or my back pressed to the whirlpool in a tub of hot water the comparison becomes reasonable.

We leave the locker room with a clap of hands, pass between the tan burlap curtains under the loge seats and onto the hardwood surface of Madison Square Garden. The spotlights shining down from the spoked-wheel ceiling make the court warm, even hot. As we form two lines for warm-up layins, the Garden audio department blasts a record whose high-speed percussion ratchets through the enormous loudspeakers hanging suspended over center court. During the first game that was played in the new Garden, in 1968, a large metal plate fell from the ceiling to the floor, and since then I have thought about what might happen if the gigantic speaker fell. The players who never get back on defense or never go for rebounds would be the most likely victims.

I approach the basket slowly, take the pass from Frazier and lay the ball against the backboard. The pace is slow and jerky. As you get older, the warm-up becomes more important. Muscles are tight and restrict movement. They need to be slowly stretched and loosened for the running and jumping to follow. A rhythm develops which puts me in tune with the game rhythm.

Before playoff games, nervousness and determination mark the faces of players. There are shouts of encouragement to teammates and glares at opponents. Each player tries to convince his body to perform beyond its capacity. But during the regular season the warm-ups are a time of hellos to opponents, smiling inquiries about families, and occasionally the making of post-game plans.

The record fades into the more familiar accompaniment of organ music. Stiff muscles yield, the tempo picks up. I see the ball drop through the hoop. I start, fake left, and then cut right, going toward the basket at an angle. The ball thuds into my hands. I feel the grain, bring the ball up to my chest, and drop it softly against the backboard. Coming down on my toes, I take five steps to slow down, then jog to the end of the rebounding line. The music plays, people watch, and a mood begins to form.

As the lay-ins draw to a close, the younger players start the playful movement of basketball, the dunk shot, literally stuffing the ball into the basket. There are many varieties. The straight one-hand and two-hand dunks are elementary. The reverse dunk, however, requires a player to approach the basket frontally and then at the last moment turn at a right angle in the air and slam the ball over the left backside of the rim with the right hand. For the hesitation dunk, a player "skies" (jumps very high). As he approaches the level of the basket, he ducks his head aside to miss the rim or net and at the last moment, after his body is past the basket but before it descends, he reaches back with one hand and stuffs the ball through. The self-assist dunk is the most violent: a player tosses the ball against the backboard and as it caroms off, he jumps, catches it above the rim and slams it through, all in one motion. With my limited jumping ability I'm not much on the dunk. The standing locker-room joke is that a daily *New York Times* can't be slipped under my feet even on my highest jump. So, in between the "oohing" and "aahing" the crowd gives for the practice dunks, I shoot driving hooks and reverse lay-ups against the glass. After my last lay-in made running flatout down the center, I go to the right corner of the court to tighten my shoelaces. A little boy and girl shout, "Dollar, look up, look up. Please. We want your picture. You're our favorite Knick." I look up, but they don't take the picture so I return to my sneakers. The two young voices call again, "Look up, look up, you jerk!" No player can blot out the comments from the crowd. He can only pretend he doesn't hear.

After the lay-ins, the team starts individual warm-up shots, using six balls. A jumper, a free throw, a hook, a running one-hander—each player will run through his repertoire until he has reaffirmed it against the imaginary opponents of the warm-up.

DeBusschere practices his long jumper from the corners and his full-speed drives across the middle to the basket. He jump-shoots three from the low post and tips in a few rebounds off the glass. Lucas stands twenty-five feet from the basket. He shoots with a piston-like motion—one bounce, fix the ball into shooting position, jump, fade, kick one leg forward, release the ball near the right ear. Monroe works on his rhythm, faking his shot, driving to the basket, pulling up for the jumper from the hip. Frazier dribbles from baseline to halfcourt five times. I shoot fouls and take jumpers at points on the court where our plays are designed to spring me for the open shot.

Muscles loosen even more and confidence grows. Sometimes you can sink every shot in the warm-ups, but the shots in the game fail to drop. Other times just the reverse. Each player has his own superstitions: taking the last shot, swishing the last shot, walking to the bench last or first, shooting with one ball only, saying hello to a friend in the stands.

Frazier and DeBusschere rarely use the full ten minutes for shooting; they prefer to sit on the bench for two or three minutes, thinking about their opponent.

Several years ago, I took to surveying the crowd for lovely women, and now in Madison Square Garden three women are part of my pregame fantasy ritual. They sit in different places and they attend games often. At some point during the warm-ups, I will stare at each of the three. I don't want to meet them and I'm sure they aren't aware of their strange role in my preparation. After two years, one of them made it known through friends that she was available, but somehow it didn't seem right. From what I saw, she was extremely attractive and alluring; meeting her might dispel that image. I knew she was bound to be different. Anyway, I did not want to find out, because the very act of meeting her would destroy the role she played in my warm-ups. So, I continued just to look. She caught my glances with recognition for several more months, but finally ignored me altogether. I still notice her dress, her hair, and the remarkably impassive manner with which she regards the scene. Three times I have seen her from a cab walking down a New York street. She looked the same, but her allure was less, insufficient without the Garden and the game.

The buzzer sounds, indicating that players should return to their benches for the start of the game. Players take last-second shots not unlike students cramming, minutes before an exam.

"Welcome to the magical world of Madison Square Garden," says John Condon, the Garden's public address announcer, "where tonight it's the New York Knicks against the Los Angeles Lakers. And now for the Los Angeles starting lineup . . ."

"Boooooo." The Garden vibrates like a bass violin string. Few opposing teams escape the New York boo.

"Now the World Champion New York Knicks . . ."

Sound of waterfalls, a continuous roar.

"Playing forward, No. 22, Dave DeBusschere."

Waterfalls.

"Playing forward, No. 24, Bill Bradley."

Waterfalls.

"Playing center, No. 32, Jerry Lucas."

More waterfalls.

DeBusschere and I stand stonefaced as the remaining introductions are made. DeBusschere says, "I found her. I'm playing for her tonight."

"Where, which one?" I ask.

"The blonde in the blue sweater up to the right of Gate 13."

I glance up the wall of faces, past Wall Street types in their three-piece suits, past blue-jeaned bearded kids, until I focus on an unknown woman in a gray skirt and a blue turtleneck sweater. She gazes down at us as the National Anthem is announced. "Okay, we'll do it for her tonight," I say.

Each game has a pace of its own. One can never be sure of how a game will end by checking the score at halftime. I have been on teams that lost 30-point leads. I have come from 25 back to win. The score means little. What is important is being able to sense the mood of the opponent. What I feel is his will. A team sometimes gets behind 20 points and caves in; it just gives up. The team tries but its execution becomes sloppy; the players don't get back on defense as fast, or play as tenaciously against their men. They take bad shots, start to bicker among themselves, and in their ultimate discouragement talk to their opponent about their own teammates' shortcomings.

I sense tonight's game against the Lakers is over by halftime. We have a 21-point lead. During the third quarter the Lakers make their move, cutting it to 12. We hold and then increase our lead to 18. With six minutes gone in the third quarter, I know we have it.

For the rest of the third quarter, I just watch Frazier. Occasionally he infuriates me when he doesn't pass the ball as much as I would like, and DeBusschere sometimes, after running six times up the floor without getting a shot, will throw up his arms in anger and shout "pass the god damn ball." But there is no denying Clyde's ability. I am on the same court but I'm a spectator. He plays with smooth and effortless grace, as if he were a dancer revealing the beauty of a body in movement. It's somehow right that he doesn't sweat much. His build is perfect for basketball: tall, erect, and thin. He can move with deceptive speed. The jumper, its fake, and the drive are his repertoire—he does not have a lot of moves like Monroe. He is classic in his economy of motion, though an occasional behind-the-back dribble shows there is still a flirtation with flamboyance. Holzman says that people should get to see him practice, for that's where he plays complete basketball. Tonight he's doing a pretty good job of it on Los Angeles. He shoulder fakes and hits two jumpers; a third time he draws the foul, and follows with a baseline drive and a fade-away, at which several players on the Los Angeles bench shake their heads in awe. The next time downcourt he uses a change of pace dribble that makes the defensive man look ridiculous: Tonight he could make anyone look bad.

The crowd excitement at games brings out Clyde's supreme efforts. "It's like dancing," he says. "When you hear a certain record you dance and you can feel it. That's the same way I feel about the roar of crowds. They help me get psyched up. If the game is tied in the last five minutes and I make a basket, I'm telling myself, 'You're ready now, Clyde. Now you're going to come up with the steal, or get the rebound, or make three more baskets.' "

Toward the end of the game Frazier makes three steals and two difficult drives. He finishes with 44 points and wins the knitted shirts as star of the game.

"Why were you so hot?" asked one reporter.

"Is this your best effort of the year?"

"What are you wearing tonight, Clyde?"

"Are the Knicks going to catch the Celtics?"

"Let's go," says Whelan. "The bus leaves in ten minutes."

There is terror behind the dream of being a professional ballplayer. It comes as a slow realization of finality and of the frightening unknowns which the end brings. When the playing is over, one can sense that one's youth has been spent playing a game and now both the game and youth are gone, along with the innocence that characterizes all games which at root are pure and promote a prolonged adolescence in those who play. Now the athlete must face a world where awkward naiveté can no longer be overlooked because of athletic performance. By age thirty-five any potential for developing skills outside of basketball is slim. The "good guy" syndrome ceases. What is left is the other side of the Faustian bargain: To live all one's days never able to recapture the feeling of those few years of intensified youth. In a way it is the fate of a warrior class to receive rewards, plaudits, and exhilaration simultaneously with the means of self-destruction. When a middle-aged lawyer moves more slowly on the tennis court, he makes adjustments and may even laugh at his geriatric restrictions because for him there remains the law. For the athlete who reaches thirty-five, something in him dies; not a peripheral activity but a fundamental passion. It necessarily dies. The athlete rarely recuperates. He approaches the end of his playing days the way old people approach death. He puts his finances in order. He reminisces easily. He offers advice to the young. But, the athlete differs from an old person in that he must continue living. Behind all the years of practice and all the hours of glory waits that inexorable terror of living without the game.

Nancy Lieberman-Cline with Debby Jennings

From Lady Magic

When Dean Meminger called me and asked if I wanted to play in the USBL in the summer of 1987, I was ready to go out and have a good time playing basketball. Stan Goldman, the owner of the Long Island Knights, flew to Dallas and visited with me about the team. I was excited about playing basketball again and signed a three-year contract with the Knights.

On paper, we had a really solid team, with Micheal Ray Richardson and Geoff Huston as two of our top players. Dean, who had persuaded me to go to Dallas to talk to the Diamonds owners in 1980, was the coach of the Knights.

Micheal Ray and I were real close. The only thing keeping him out of the NBA was that he'd had some drug problems, and I was his unofficial babysitter that summer. Dean made it my job to keep him away from drugs, because he was tested every week, and to keep him away from women, too.

When I got into a fight, I always knew Micheal was right there. "Baby, ain't nobody gonna hurt you." Once I got into a confrontation with Andre Turner. I have the ball, and I'm trying to pass, and he's right up in my face, so I take the ball and—boom!—I hit the ball off his forehead. He started yelling and screaming and cursing at me, and I said, "Why don't you just cut the crap and play ball and stop whining like a girl?"

"I ain't no girl," he said.

"You're 5–8, you're 160 pounds, got a high voice, and you tell me you're not like a girl?" So we get into this shoving match, and all of a sudden Micheal Ray comes in and—boom! And Micheal Ray and Geoff Huston are saying, "Are you OK, baby? Are you OK?" They were just so good to me, so protective.

The hardest thing about traveling in the USBL, which was the first time I ever had to go on the road with men, was that you never knew where your locker room was. In some arenas I'd have a locker down the road. Sometimes I had to get my own area in the shower. The guys were really good to me; they were never lewd or anything like that.

I will say, though, that all some of these guys talk about on the road is who they've slept with, groupies, maids in the room, whomever. I remember one five-hour bus ride and this one player who spent the whole trip talking about one escapade, leaving nothing to the imagination. I looked at Dean Meminger and said, "He's been talking about this for five hours. I cannot believe that is the only thing this man has thought about for five hours." And everybody listening to him was like, "Yeah!" "Right!" "Oh, yeah!" It was like everybody was trying to prove their manhood to each other.

I always enjoyed playing in the USBL because the guys

in the league were steps away from a team in Europe, the Continental Basketball Association, or the NBA. Many of them had played previously in one of those leagues and were back trying to get the attention of the owners and general managers. These leagues are basketball's minors, and impressions are made and forgotten quickly.

One time we were in the locker room, getting ready to play against Tyrone Bogues' team. Tyrone's a big fan favorite, of course, because he's only 5-foot-3, but he's one of the quickest guys around. All the other players are always scared to death of getting embarrassed by someone so little.

So Micheal Ray is trying to fire up the guys in the locker room, saying stuff like, "I don't care how big he is, he comes near me, forearm to the head. I don't care how little he is." And Geoff Huston's joining in: "We'll kill the dude! He comes down the lane, boom!" All these guys are talking about what they're going to do to Bogues.

When the game starts, Micheal's saying, "I'm gonna post him up." First time Micheal gets the ball down on the post, he goes to make his move, and Tyrone strips the ball from him and takes off down the court. We're on the bench yelling, "Micheal, post him up, baby!" Next time down, he goes to post him up, and—zip!—there goes Tyrone the other way with the ball again. "Keep posting him up, Micheal Ray!" Finally Micheal just walks over to Meminger and says, "Take me out of the game, I ain't guarding that little son of a bitch!"

Everybody on the bench is just sitting there laughing and Dean says, "Nancy." "Huh?" "Go in the game for Micheal Ray." "Who am I gonna guard?" "Bogues." "Hey, *I* wasn't mouthing off about him before the game—I respected him!" Dean says, "Would you just shut up and get in the game?"

So I get in the game, and Tyrone is dribbling the ball, and Geoff Huston is forcing him to the sideline and we're trying to trap him before he gets to halfcourt. Tyrone goes to spin and I steal the ball from him. He is just surprised as can be. I'm coming down the left side, with my left hand to make the layup. I go up with the ball—and Tyrone can jump, he's got like a 40-plus-inch vertical leap—he goes up, and I just put the ball back behind my back and drop it off for Huston to make the layup.

The crowd goes nuts, and Tyrone just turns around to me and says, "That was a *damn* nice move!" "Thank you, Tyrone. Can I call you Mugsy?" After that, he really respected the fact that, one, I stole the ball from him and, two, he thought he had it blocked because I had held it up in front of me as long as I could, and at the last minute I dropped it off, and Geoff made the shot. Of course, Micheal's on the bench yelling, "You're so lucky!"

In order to play against guys, I always had to be mentally and physically ready. Some of those guys would come in to practice, they'd been drinking, they hadn't been asleep in two days, but they were so physically gifted that the next night they'd play and score 40 points. It would just drive me nuts. I'd drink V-8 juice and go to sleep at 10 o'clock and say my prayers and lead a clean life, and I'd go out there and these guys are bigger, quicker, faster, stronger—there's nothing that I could have done to compete on an equal footing.

So every day in practice, I'd be ready and keyed up—I couldn't afford mental lapses because I had physical shortcomings to deal with. But they knew every time I stepped on the court, I was ready to play or practice, and they respected that.

Cameron Stauth

"The Pistons"
From The Franchise

Two young men, one black and one white, both tall, shot baskets in a cold, shadowy field house in Windsor, Ontario, just across the Detroit River from downtown Detroit. They were remarkably skilled. The ball was light in their hands and they feathered it through the net so softly that it barely ripped the strings. One would stand deep in the corner sinking shots in rhythmical cadence while the other rebounded, then they would switch places. With obvious pleasure, they would drift into dancing sets of one-on-one. They seemed almost never to miss, and when they did miss they would leap after the ball and ram it through the rim with violent grace. Every so often, they would punctuate their play with a trick shot—bouncing the ball off the floor into the basket, or standing with their backs to the hoop and flipping it up backward.

At the other end of the court, an older man tossed up hook shots. He wasn't particularly good, but he seemed to be enjoying himself. Sitting near him, just off the court, a very large black man teased him, offering advice and criticism, making jokes. Sometimes the older man paid attention, and sometimes he didn't.

Then there was a stirring in the gym and the sound of deep voices and heavy footsteps. A line of men in shorts and T-shirts emerged from a runway that led to the locker room. They were, unmistakably, professional basketball players.

On television, or even from a tenth-row seat in a stadium, professional basketball players look like other athletes—tall and muscular. But that's the view from a distance, and from the perspective of seeing them next to one another. Up close, and from one's own perspective, they are the most physically remarkable people in the world.

To a basketball fan, seven feet no longer sounds exceptionally tall. It's basically the minimum height for a center. Ralph Sampson and Mark Eaton are seven feet, four inches, and Manute Bol is seven-seven. But the eyes of a relatively tall man—someone six-one or six-two—hit a seven-footer in the middle of his chest. A six-footer must crane his neck to look at a seven-footer like a child looking at an adult. And much more than height, it is size that sets pro basketball players apart. Every part of a man who is six-eight to seven feet is of unusual proportion: hands, neck, arms, feet—even eyes and ears. Hands are like baseball gloves, eyes can be as huge and round as those of a stallion, and arms are stacked with muscle and are long as tree limbs. All this size and strength, though, is carried with the silky grace of a professional dancer. Because of this unusual combination of size, strength, and grace, pro basketball players are often called "the best athletes in the world." Their physical presence—which they have been trained to expand for intimidation—is overpowering. And in a group—even a relaxed, quiet group like the one that was loping into the gym in Windsor—the collective physical presence is unparalleled.

"Okay!" yelled the older man—Detroit Piston coach Chuck Daly—"Everybody off the floor but players! Dawkins, let's go!" The large black man who'd been teasing Daly eased out of the stands, and the two men at the other end of the court put down their ball and took a seat in the bleachers. They were high school basketball coaches who'd come to watch the big time. Skilled as these two men were, they were no better than one million other young men at the game of basketball. The men who were gathering around Daly, though, were of a wholly different category. They were among the 250 best basketball players in the world. They all moved with a sense of strength, gracefulness, confidence—and arrogance—that is present only in the movements of a few hundred men.

Even some of the players—the rookies—were in awe of their colleagues. Now that the season was approaching, only the best young prospects had been allowed to join the members of last year's team for fall camp. Most of the players from rookie camp were long gone. Only Dave Popson and six others have survived McCloskey's first cut.

Daly and McCloskey were ready to get down to serious business. But to Michael Williams, McCloskey's second pick in last summer's college draft, the situation had an odd, dreamlike quality. Just three months ago, in late June, Williams had been watching these players fight for the World

Championship on television. Now they stood on either side of him, and he felt not as if his dreams had become real, but as if he'd jumped into the television, and were just watching his dream from another angle. He couldn't possibly feel like he'd achieved his dream of playing in the NBA, because he still had to survive the final roster cuts. Right now there were seventeen players gathered around Daly, and only twelve would make the team. To earn a spot, Williams would have to win the approval of McCloskey, who, as general manager, had authority over all personnel decisions. McCloskey wasn't on the floor with Daly. He was in the stands, watching quietly. Always watching. Williams's agent, Bill Blakely, had not been able to persuade McCloskey to guarantee Williams's $100,000 salary, the league minimum. That put Williams at a significant disadvantage, because McCloskey had nothing invested in him. Williams had been chosen in the second round as the forty-eighth pick, and picks that low virtually never got guaranteed salaries.

That disadvantage was a cruel twist of fate for Williams, because McCloskey had actually been more interested in Williams than he'd been in Detroit's first pick, Wyoming guard Fennis Dembo, who *had* gotten a guaranteed salary.

Williams's future had become threatened because of publicity. Dembo had made the cover of *Sports Illustrated* last year—getting the attention of everybody in the league. Williams, playing in relative obscurity at Baylor, had gained little national attention. But McCloskey had seen things in Williams that others hadn't. McCloskey had a reputation for uncovering diamonds in the rough, and he had been willing to stake that reputation on Williams. But he'd gambled. He'd wanted both Dembo and Williams, so he'd taken Dembo first, hoping that no one else valued Williams as much as he did. The gamble had paid off. Williams had still been available at the forty-eighth pick.

But once McCloskey had gotten Williams, he hadn't given him a guaranteed salary. Simple reason. He didn't have to. Williams didn't have the bargaining power to demand it.

So now Williams was having to scrap his way onto the team. He was doing a good job of it, though. He'd played well in rookie camp, and had then made the All-League Team of the NBA's Summer League, which had just concluded. At first, Williams had been shocked at the skill level in the Summer League, a preseason proving ground for rookies and free agents. Williams was only six-two and 175 pounds—slight by NBA standards—but he was bullet-fast and had blown right past everyone in college. In the Summer League, however, players six-nine and 225 were blowing past *him*. He'd seen players like that on television and had thought he was ready for them. But TV just didn't convey it: the ungodly whoosh of a huge player whistling past like a semi. You couldn't prepare for that—you just endured it.

At the moment, Williams was bringing the ball downcourt. Daly had split them into two groups for a scrimmage. There was no time to screw around with orientation and conditioning drills and pep talks—McCloskey would make his final roster cuts in a couple of weeks. It was time to try to become a millionaire—the average salary in the league was about $500,000, and in about twenty months, when the new TV contract kicked in, it was expected to rise to $1 million per year. If the rookies didn't become millionaires, they'd drop back into the real world—the world of the two high school coaches who'd been shooting baskets. The NBA was an all-

or-nothing proposition, because America really had no minor leagues. There was only the Continental Basketball Association, and its players made less than high school coaches. The real minors were the colleges, and they didn't pay—at least not after four years.

Williams eyed the defense—Isiah Thomas was guarding him, and Bill Laimbeer and Rick Mahorn were under the hoop. The prudent move: pass off to Adrian Dantley. But that wasn't the way into the league. First and last, the NBA was a shooter's league. If you couldn't shoot the ball . . . Williams ducked his head and drove toward Laimbeer. He flew into the air with the ball in front of him. He had a clear shot off the glass. Then: *bash!* Laimbeer, seventy pounds heavier and nine inches taller than Williams, shifted suddenly and heaved his weight into Williams, knocking him to the floor so hard he bounced twice. Williams lay on the floor, feeling dizzy and sick as pain shuddered up and down his body. Trainer Mike Abdenouor ran up and put his hand on Williams's arm to keep him from getting up. But Williams wasn't going anywhere. He was spread-eagled and choking for breath. Laimbeer turned and walked away. No apology: Welcome to the NBA. For about two minutes, Williams lay panting and twitching. Gradually, he worked his way upright, then found the free-throw line. His right hand was beginning to throb and turn purple, but he didn't favor it. He didn't want to show anyone he was hurting. He just wanted to make his free throws. He wasn't trying to impress McCloskey or Daly. It was instinct. But it was the instinct that McCloskey had drafted him for.

After the scrimmage, Isiah Thomas approached Williams. "You know," said Thomas, "if you're going in on a big guy like that, you got to know how to protect yourself. In college, you just *go.* You jump over them, and you dunk on them. But at this level, everybody's so much bigger and so much stronger and so much taller that you got to find ways to protect your *body* while you get your shot off. That's why even a guy like Michael Jordan—he can jump over a *lot* of people—but he turns his back to a guy while he's in the air, and then flips it over his shoulder. That's to protect his *body.*"

Williams was grateful, not just for the advice but for the attention. But he didn't react effusively. That wouldn't be cool. Besides, he was worried. His hand was getting fatter and more blue by the minute, and trainer Mike Abdenour had told him he'd better get it X-rayed. If it was broken, he was in trouble. They didn't save roster spots for forty-eighth picks. McCloskey would probably be sympathetic. Then he'd go out and find another body.

Jack McCallum

"Unforgettable"

Six-foot-nine-inch giants are not supposed to be able to handle the ball well enough to play guard. But the 6′9″ Magic Johnson handled it as well as anyone who ever lived. No player is supposed to have talents varied enough to enable him to play every position in the NBA. But Johnson, primarily a point guard during his 12-year career, dominated the decisive game of the 1980 Finals from the *center* position and from time to time over the last few seasons played All-Star-caliber post-up small forward and power forward.

Shooters are supposed to be born, not made. But Johnson, a nonshooter with an ugly-looking release as a collegian at Michigan State, gradually turned himself into a feared outside threat, not to mention one of the best free throw shooters in the league. And in the grind of an 82-game schedule and an enervating, pressure-packed post-season, no one is supposed to have both the playing skills and the interpersonal skills necessary to hold the reins of leadership year after year. But Johnson became the leader of the Los Angeles Lakers when he and his wide smile first walked through the doors of The Forum in 1979, and he was the team's unqualified leader when he walked away from the game, still smiling, last Thursday afternoon.

That aspect of Johnson's career—his leadership—will perhaps be his greatest legacy as a player, and it goes well beyond mere popularity. The most successful NBA teams are those with a personality, an identity, and the Lakers have been consistent winners since 1979 largely because they knew who they were: They were Magic's team, pure and simple. Late in a game, there was no question about who would direct traffic and determine the best final shot, as there sometimes was on, say, the Boston Celtics, whose leader, Larry Bird, was not their primary ball handler. Johnson dictated when the Lakers ran and when they walked, when they got it inside to Kareem Abdul-Jabbar and when they pitched it back out for a Byron Scott jumper. He knew where James Worthy liked the ball on the break and when Vlade Divac had to be whacked on the backside and told to rebound.

In fact there were times in recent years when Magic quite literally talked his team through its paces during games, giving the Lakers, in effect, the NBA's only voice-operated offense. *O.K., James, give it back, cut through now, rub off A.C., O.K., post up. . . .* It was quite audible even to the reporters on press row, not to mention the defense, but Magic's theory was that if you did something right, it didn't matter who knew it was coming.

His leadership in the locker room was equally important. After Game 2 of the 1987 NBA Finals, in which the Lakers demolished the Celtics 141–122 to take a 2–0 series lead, veteran Laker guard Michael Cooper, a great talker, was rambling on to reporters long after the game. That was customarily Magic's role too, and he performed it with great aplomb. But on this night Magic, who dressed next to Cooper, was concerned that his team would be lulled into complacency by two easy victories.

"O.K., Coop, wrap it up," Magic whispered to Cooper.

But the questions kept coming, and Cooper kept talking. Magic tapped him on the shoulder. "Coop!" he said. "I said that's it. Now!"

Cooper smiled, shrugged his shoulders and said to the reporters, "Well, you heard him."

For a dozen years Magic had the Lakers under his thumb. And they loved being there.

What set Magic apart on the court? His height, of course, an advantage at the guard position that cannot be overstated. In a league where the best teams have come to rely more and more on sophisticated defenses, the Lakers were virtually untrappable because Magic was able to throw the ball over defenders. The simple entry pass to the post was no trouble for him, as it is for so many NBA guards who are susceptible to the thievery of quick-handed defenders like the Milwaukee Bucks' Alvin Robertson and the Chicago Bulls' Michael Jordan.

This is not to say that Magic dominated his position for 12 years simply because he was taller than everyone else. He also threw the ball *under* defenses about as well as anyone who ever played the game. How many times did you see Magic grab a defensive rebound, take a few dribbles upcourt—"powering out," as Pat Riley called it when he coached the Lakers—and throw an indescribable 40-foot bullet of a bounce pass that met Worthy or Scott in full stride, just as they cut toward the basket? That ability to calculate the convergence of a bouncing ball with a sprinting player is a gift, and Magic is one of the few players who ever had it.

In addition to his height, Magic's strength and pure bulk (he weighed at least 220 pounds for most of his career) were his most important physical attributes. Though he will be forever associated with the transition game, he was neither particularly fast—he moved with a kind of lumbering grace—nor as quick as many others at his position. What he was able to do was get where he wanted to go, not more quickly but much more efficiently than anyone else. On the break his dribbling skills took him around defenders who challenged him early, and his spin move remained unequaled even in 1991. And once he got into the lane, it was all over: He simply bulled his way to the basket.

In the half-court game Magic's bulk was a formidable factor, and at times, as he maneuvered smaller and slighter backcourt opponents like the Phoenix Suns' Kevin Johnson and the Utah Jazz's John Stockton closer and closer to the basket, he looked like a father toying with his sons out in the driveway.

Riley, who coached Magic for nine years, always thought Johnson's nickname was unfortunate in some respects, suggesting as it did a smoke-and-mirrors quality that diverted attention from the fundamental soundness of Johnson's game. (Riley always called Johnson by either his given name, Earvin, or Buck, another nickname.) There is something to that, for Magic was never quite as fancy or tricky as that moniker suggests. Some two decades before Johnson came into the league, Bob Cousy put the ball between his legs and around his back much more frequently than Magic would.

What defined the Lakers' Showtime fast-break style at its zenith was the way Magic sold his moves from the middle of the floor. Magic surely has the most expressive face in the history of sports. As he steamed toward the basket, his eyes would widen and his mouth would round into an O as he looked off his defender, selling the pass to, say, Scott on the right side and then suddenly zipping it over his shoulder to Worthy on the left. The fast break is about making decisions in the wink of an eye, and Magic, like vintage Cousy, made excellent ones while earning thousands of style points in the process.

Ultimately, the unique thing about Johnson as a player is that he was able to be at the cutting edge while still being somewhat old-fashioned. Until he slowed down a bit in recent seasons, he was the consummate playground player—the high dribble, the spin moves, the outside shot that looked like an afterthought. But even in his most electrifying moments he was, in contrast to Jordan, never a particularly acrobatic player or a great leaper, especially as his knees grew more tender. Like Bird, that other noted relic, he never had a classic jump shot, relying instead on an anachronistic one-hand set. And as the years rolled on, his signature shot became the hook, that hoary creation that he, like players of old, took—and made—with either hand. In deference to Abdul-Jabbar, he called it "the junior, junior skyhook." Magic was never just like Jordan, never just like Bird. He was somewhere in between, and thus attracted fans from both camps.

Like all superstars, Magic got favorable treatment from referees. There were hundreds of times when he could have been called for charging on the fast break, when he leaned in and simply overpowered a defender with that big body. And there were thousands of other occasions when he could have been whistled for traveling, when he took an extra step or two on his way to the basket. But the NBA has become a refuge for stylists, a place where the great players are allowed to be great. And few in the history of the game have been greater than Johnson.

Ira Berkow

"To Hoops On Its 100th"

I sent a Christmas gift recently to the Springfield, Mass., Y.M.C.A. It was a basketball. This doesn't exactly make me Kris Kringle, but it was the least I could do.

I've been playing basketball ever since grammar school, ever since high school, ever since college, and still haven't stopped. I understood Isiah Thomas when he mentioned in an interview why he had built a basketball court in his house. "Do you play anything else? Golf, say, or tennis?" he was asked. "No," he said. "Maybe one day. But, really, any chance I get, I play basketball. I'm still a hooper at heart." There are many levels of hoopers, from Isiah on down to—well, just on down.

Not long ago I was in Springfield on assignment and, knowing that the 100th anniversary of the game would soon be commemorated there at the Basketball Hall of Fame, I brought my hoop gear (somehow, I usually manage to find room in my bags for it) to the Springfield Y.

It was my first trip to that modest mecca where basketball originated, on or about Dec. 21, 1891. Dr. James Naismith had been charged by his boss at the Springfield Y training school to develop an indoor game so students could get exercise during wintertime. Doc twitched his mustache with disdain, for he had other things to tend to, but then did as ordered. Up went a pair of peach baskets on the balcony, which happened to be 10 feet above the gym there. The next thing we know—100 years later—basketballs are bouncing all over the world.

Basketball may be played and seen and agonized over (note all the newspaper photos of tearful cheerleaders when their teams have lost) and loved by more people in more places than any other sport in history.

I paid a $10 fee at the Y and asked for a basketball. The woman behind the counter handed me a rubber ball with a bump in it. I asked for a ball without a bump, and a leather one. Rubber is for outdoor use, as everyone knows, leather for indoor. She had about six other balls. "They're all rubber, except for this one," she said, holding a worn leather ball in both hands. "But this has a flap on it." In fact, there was a loose tear in one of the strips on the ball.

"I'll take the one with the flap," I said, with a shrug.

How nice, I thought, that after 100 years the Springfield Y still has all the same balls that Naismith invented the game with.

Some things had changed, however. For one, this was a new building. And Naismith would never recognize the gym. No balcony, no peach baskets. Instead, glass backboards and a large wooden floor with colorful lines gleamed in the well-lighted room. Two young men were shooting at one basket. They invited me to play. I said yes. "Hey," said a guy who had just come in, "can I run wichyoo." Sure, I said.

We played with the ball with the flap, which was the best ball we had. We picked, we screened, we tried to hit a cutter, we took a bad shot, we made a surprising one—and heard the sweet snap of the net—we stole a ball, we lost one. There was a dispute. It was resolved. Play resumed.

The half-court game was reminiscent of basketball games I've played and watched, mostly with pleasure, for years. It is a lesson in human nature. It is not just who passes how, for example, but when—from playground to pro. It is beyond skill. It has to do with character, and characters, and I've personally known many, from one called Junior Jive (or just J.J.), a fancy young player who threw behind-the-back passes into the wall, to one named Monster, for his lummox game (and if you called his home and asked one of his kids for their father, they'd holler, "Monster—telephone!").

One is also known by the calls he makes in a pickup game—or doesn't make. Once, at a Y in Manhattan, two jerks—pals—argued for a dumb call and then quit in a huff. "There goes flotsam and jetsam," said one of the remaining players. Perfect.

I once took a small, 11-year-old boy named Timmy to meet his idol, Calvin Murphy, the Houston Rockets' short star. In Murphy's hotel room, the conversation ranged from sneakers to grades. Murphy then helped Timmy on with his coat, and asked to see his jump shot. Timmy readily complied, with his left-handed J. Soon after, Timmy said he was disappointed. "If I hadn't been wearing my coat," he said, "I could really have soared."

Hoopers like Timmy and Calvin, meanwhile, also know that the best indoor ball is a leather one without a flap, and with a good grainy feel and grooves. That's why I had to send one to the Springfield Y. In appreciation.

Merry Christmas, Basketball, and Happy 100th.

JOHN EDGAR WIDEMAN
"Michael Jordan Leaps the Great Divide" from *Esquire* (November 1990). By permission of Wylie, Aiken & Stone Literary Agents.

JOHN UPDIKE
Excerpt from *Rabbit, Run* copyright 1960 by John Updike. Reprinted by permission of Alfred A. Knopf, Inc.

PAT CONROY
Excerpt from *The Great Santini* copyright 1976 by Pat Conroy. Reprinted by permission of Houghton Mifflin Company.

ROBERT GREENFIELD
Excerpt from *Haymon's Crowd* copyright by Robert Greenfield. Reprinted by permission of the author.

RICK TELANDER
Excerpt from *Heaven Is a Playground* copyright 1976 by Rick Telander. Reprinted by permission of Simon & Schuster.

RON SHELTON
Excerpt from "White Men Can't Jump" copyright by Ron Shelton. Reprinted by permission of Fox Studios.

PETE AXTHELM
"The Fallen Idol: The Harlem Tragedy of Earl Manigault" from *The City Game* copyright 1970 by Pete Axthelm. Reprinted by permission of Sterling Lord Literistic, Inc.

IAN O'CONNOR
"A King Felled by Drugs Revisits Court He Ruled" copyright 1989 The New York Times Company. Reprinted by permission.

DAVID O. WEBER
"American Pastime" originally appeared in *Evergreen Review*, November 1970. Copyright a 1970 by Evergreen Review, Inc. Used by permission of Grove Press, Inc.

THOMAS A. BOSWELL
"The Shooter" from *Gameday* copyright 1990 by Washington Post Writers Group. Reprinted by permission of Doubleday, a division of Bantam Doubleday Dell Publishing Group, Inc.

PHILIP ROTH

Excerpt from *Goodbye, Columbus* copyright 1959 renewed 1987 by Philip Roth. Reprinted by permission of Houghton Mifflin Company.

JOHN FEINSTEIN

Excerpt from *A Season on the Brink: A Year with Bobby Knight and the Indiana Hoosiers* copyright 1986 by John Feinstein. Reprinted by permission of Macmillan Publishing Company.

BOB COUSY and JOHN DEVANEY

Excerpt from *The Killer Instinct* copyright 1975 by Robert Cousy and John Devaney. Reprinted by permission of Random House, Inc.

DAVID HALBERSTAM

Excerpt from *The Breaks of the Game* copyright 1981 by David Halberstam. Reprinted by permission of Alfred A. Knopf, Inc.

DAVE ANDERSON

"Good-by to Jerry West" copyright 1974 by The New York Times Company. Reprinted by permission.

JOHN McPHEE

"Coliseum Hour" copyright 1966 The New Yorker Magazine, Inc. Reprinted by permission.

BOB RYAN and TERRY PLUTO

Excerpt from *Forty-Eight Minutes* copyright 1987 by Terry Pluto and Bob Ryan. Reprinted with permission by Macmillan Publishing Company.

WILLIAM GOLDMAN and MIKE LUPICA

"Revolution Comes to Madison Square" from *Wait Till Next Year* copyright 1988 by William Goldman and Mike Lupica. Reprinted with permission of Bantam Books, a division of Bantam Doubleday Dell Publishing Group, Inc.

BILL BRADLEY

Excerpt from *Life on the Run,* copyright 1978 by Bill Bradley. Reprinted with the permission of the author.

NANCY LIEBERMAN-CLINE

Excerpt from *Lady Magic* copyright 1991 by Nancy Lieberman-Cline with Debbie Jennings. Reprinted with the permission of the author.

CAMERON STAUTH

Excerpt from *The Franchise* copyright 1990 by Cameron Stauth. Reprinted by permission of William Morrow & Company, Inc.

JACK McCALLUM

The following article is reprinted courtesy of *Sports Illustrated* from the November 18, 1991 issue. Copyright 1991, Time Inc. ("Unforgettable" by Jack McCallum.) All rights reserved.

IRA BERKOW

"Sports of The Times; To Hoops On Its 100th," by Ira Berkow, December 25, 1991. Copyright 1991 by The New York Times Company. Reprinted by permission.

D.C. PUBLIC LIBRARY
3 1172 03265 7694